Company's Coming®

MUFFINS & MORE

by
Jean Paré

Cover Photo

MUFFINS & MORE

Fifteenth Edition September, 1990

I.S.B.N. 0-9690695-2-9

Published and Distributed by
Company's Coming Publishing Limited
Box 8037, Station "F"
Edmonton, Alberta, Canada
T6H 4N9

Printed in Canada

Cookbooks in the Company's Coming series by Jean Paré:

Soft Cover Titles

150 DELICIOUS SQUARES*
(Also available in French)

COOKIES

CASSEROLES

VEGETABLES

MUFFINS & MORE

MAIN COURSES

SALADS

PASTA

APPETIZERS

CAKES

DESSERTS

BARBECUES (APRIL, 1991)

SOUPS & SANDWICHES

HOLIDAY ENTERTAINING

Hard Cover Title

JEAN PARÉ'S FAVORITES
VOLUME ONE

Cookbooks in the Jean Paré series (French):

Soft Cover Title

150 DÉLICIEUX CARRÉS*

table of Contents

the Jean Paré story

Jean Paré was born and raised during the Great Depression in Irma, a small rural town in eastern Alberta, Canada. She grew up understanding that the combination of family, friends and home cooking is the essence of a good life. Jean learned from her mother, Ruby Elford, to appreciate good cooking and was encouraged by her father, Edward Elford, who praised even her earliest attempts. When she left home she took with her many acquired family recipes, her love of cooking and her intriguing desire to read recipe books like novels!

While raising a family of four, Jean was always busy in her kitchen preparing delicious, tasty treats and savory meals for family and friends of all ages. Her reputation flourished as the mom who would happily feed the neighborhood.

In 1963, when her children had all reached school age, Jean volunteered to cater to the 50th anniversary of the Vermilion School of Agriculture, now Lakeland College. Working out of her home, Jean prepared a dinner for over 1000 people which launched a flourishing catering operation that continued for over eighteen years. During that time she was provided with countless opportunities to test new ideas with immediate feedback — resulting in empty plates and contented customers! Whether preparing cocktail sandwiches for a house party or serving a hot meal for 1500 people, Jean Paré earned a reputation for good food, courteous service and reasonable prices.

"Why don't you write a cookbook?" Time and again, as requests for her recipes mounted, Jean was asked that question. Jean's response was to team up with her son Grant Lovig in the fall of 1980 to form Company's Coming Publishing Limited. April 14, 1981 marked the debut of "150 DELICIOUS SQUARES", the first Company's Coming cookbook in what soon would become Canada's most popular cookbook series. Jean released a new title each year for the first six years. The pace quickened and by 1987 the company had begun publishing two titles each year.

Jean Paré's operation has grown from the early days of working out of a spare bedroom in her home to operating a large and fully equipped test kitchen in Vermilion, Alberta near the home she and her husband Larry built. Full time staff has grown steadily to include marketing personnel located in major cities across Canada. Home office is located in Edmonton, Alberta where distribution, accounting and administration functions are headquartered. Company's Coming cookbooks are now distributed throughout Canada and the United States plus numerous overseas markets. Translation of the series to the Spanish and French languages began in 1990.

Jean Paré's approach to cooking has always called for easy to follow recipes using mostly common, affordable ingredients. Her wonderful collection of time-honored recipes, many of which are family heirlooms, are a welcome addition to any kitchen. That's why we say: taste the tradition.

To family and friends, and to hopes
that this, my third cookbook, is worthy of
their constant support and encouragement.

Foreword

With everyone so busy now–a–days it is difficult to find enough time to bake as often as we would like. Hurray for quickbreads! They are so quick and easy. No yeast required! Only common affordable ingre- dients are needed when baking any of the muffins, loaves, biscuits or other quickbreads from the recipes which follow.

Note that you may choose conventional or metric measure for each recipe.

Quickbreads call for a light hand. Quickly combine (never beat) the dry and liquid ingredients. Although an average size loaf pan was used in this book, smaller pans may be used for the smaller loaves. Muffin pans vary in size. The yield given is only a guide.

Hot biscuits or muffins turn the most simple fare into a tasty delight. Loaves ripen in flavor and can be cut easier and thinner if left for at least one day.

Quickbreads freeze exceptionally well. Loaves can be taken from the freezer, several slices cut to use, then returned to the freezer until needed again. It is best not to freeze Fritters, Yorkshire pudding or Dumplings.

Continuing thanks to everyone who purchased my first book "150 DELICIOUS SQUARES" and my second book "CASSEROLES". May this third book fill the many requests for "more". Get prepared. Company's coming for "MUFFINS & MORE"!

Jean Paré

This fancy muffin is the "icing on the cake". Good.

TOPPING

Packed brown sugar	½ cup	125 mL
All purpose flour	¼ cup	50 mL
Butter or margarine	¼ cup	50 mL

In small bowl rub sugar, flour and butter until crumbly. Set aside.

All purpose flour	1½ cups	375 mL
Granulated sugar	½ cup	125 mL
Baking powder	3 tsp.	15 mL
Salt	½ tsp.	2 mL
Egg	1	1
Milk	¼ cup	60 mL
Cooking oil	¼ cup	60 mL
Shredded apple, peeled or not	¾ cup	175 mL

In mixing bowl stir flour, sugar, baking powder and salt together. Make a well in center.

In another bowl beat egg, milk and oil to blend. Stir in apple. Pour into well. Stir until just moistened. Fill muffin tins ¾ full. Sprinkle with topping. Bake in 400°F (200°C) oven for 20-25 minutes. Makes 12.

Pictured on page 17.

Three things that cannot be kept secret are love, pain and money. They soon betray themselves.

BABY APRICOT MUFFINS

An excellent, tender muffin that combines dried apricots and baby food.

All purpose flour	1¾ cups	425 mL
Granulated sugar	½ cup	125 mL
Baking powder	2 tsp.	10 mL
Baking soda	½ tsp.	2 mL
Salt	½ tsp.	2 mL
Ground dried apricots	⅓ cup	75 mL
Egg	1	1
Cooking oil	¼ cup	50 mL
Jar of baby food apricots	7½ oz.	213 mL

Measure first six dry ingredients into large bowl. Stir thoroughly. Make a well in center.

Beat egg in small bowl until frothy. Mix in oil and apricots. Pour into well. Stir just to moisten. Batter will be lumpy. Fill greased muffin pans ¾ full. Bake in 400°F (200°C) oven for 20-25 minutes. Remove from pan after 5 minutes. Makes 18.

BANANA CHIP MUFFINS

Cake like texture with the popular banana chocolate taste.

All purpose flour	1¾ cups	425 mL
Granulated sugar	½ cup	125 mL
Baking powder	3 tsp.	15 mL
Salt	½ tsp.	2 mL
Semi-sweet chocolate chips	½ cup	125 mL
Egg	1	1
Cooking oil	¼ cup	50 mL
Milk	¼ cup	50 mL
Mashed bananas (3 medium)	1 cup	250 mL

Measure first five dry ingredients into large bowl. Mix thoroughly and make a well in center.

Beat egg until frothy. Mix in oil, milk and bananas. Pour into well. Stir only to moisten. Batter will be lumpy. Fill greased muffin tins ¾ full. Bake in 400°F (200°C) oven for 20-25 minutes. Yield: 12-14 muffins.

Pictured on page 17.

BANANA BRAN MUFFINS

Delicious with a hint of chocolate. Dark and devious! The best.

All purpose flour	1 cup	250 mL
All bran cereal	1 cup	250 mL
Baking powder	1 tsp.	5 mL
Baking soda	1 tsp.	5 mL
Salt	½ tsp.	2 mL
Cocoa	2 tbsp.	30 mL
Butter or margarine	¼ cup	50 mL
Granulated sugar	½ cup	125 mL
Eggs	2	2
Sour milk (1 tsp., 5 mL, vinegar in milk)	¼ cup	50 mL
Mashed bananas (3 medium)	1 cup	250 mL

Measure all six dry ingredients into mixing bowl. Stir to combine. Make a well in center.

Cream butter, sugar and one egg until well blended. Beat in second egg. Mix in sour milk and bananas. Pour all at once into well. Mix until moistened. Ignore lumps. Fill greased muffin pans ¾ full. Bake in 400°F (200°C) oven for 20-25 minutes. Yield: 12 muffins.

BANANA MUFFINS

Mellow banana flavor.

All purpose flour	1¾ cups	425 mL
Baking soda	1 tsp.	5 mL
Salt	¼ tsp.	2 mL
Butter or margarine	½ cup	125 mL
Granulated sugar	1¼ cups	300 mL
Eggs	2	2
Sour cream	¼ cup	50 mL
Mashed bananas (3 medium)	1 cup	250 mL

Put flour, soda and salt in large bowl. Stir together. Make a well in center.

Cream butter, sugar and one egg. Beat in second egg. Mix in sour cream and bananas. Pour into well and stir to mix. Ignore lumps. Fill greased pans ¾ full. Bake in 400°F (200°C) oven for 20-25 minutes. Yield: 16 muffins.

BANANA DATE MUFFINS

Flavors combine well in this perky muffin.

All purpose flour	2 cups	500 mL
Granulated sugar	2 tbsp.	30 mL
Baking powder	3 tsp.	15 mL
Salt	1 tsp.	5 mL
Egg, beaten	1	1
Melted butter or margarine	¼ cup	50 mL
Milk	1 cup	250 mL
Chopped dates	⅔ cup	150 mL
Diced banana	⅔ cup	150 mL

Combine flour, sugar, baking powder and salt in large bowl. Stir together. Make a well in the center.

In medium size bowl beat egg until frothy. Mix in butter, milk, dates and banana. Pour into well. Stir only to moisten. Batter will be lumpy. Fill greased muffin cups ¾ full. Bake in 400°F (200°C) oven for 20-25 minutes. Let stand 5 minutes. Remove from pan. Serve warm. Makes 16.

Pictured on page 17.

BANANA OATMEAL MUFFINS

Tender and scrumptious.

All purpose flour	1½ cups	375 mL
Rolled oats	1 cup	250 mL
Granulated sugar	½ cup	125 mL
Baking powder	2 tsp.	10 mL
Baking soda	1 tsp.	5 mL
Salt	½ tsp.	2 mL
Eggs	2	2
Cooking oil	¼ cup	50 mL
Milk	¼ cup	50 mL
Mashed bananas (3 medium)	1 cup	250 mL

(continued on next page)

In large bowl measure in first six dry ingredients. Stir to mix. Make a well in the center.

In small bowl beat eggs until frothy. Mix in oil, milk and bananas. Pour into well. Stir just to moisten. Batter will be lumpy. Fill greased muffin cups ¾ full. Bake in 400°F (200°C) oven for 20-25 minutes. Makes 12-18.

Pictured on page 17.

BLUEBERRY MUFFINS

An old favorite.

All purpose flour	1¾ cups	425 mL
Baking powder	3 tsp.	15 mL
Salt	½ tsp.	2 mL
Butter or margarine	¼ cup	50 mL
Granulated sugar	½ cup	125 mL
Egg	1	1
Milk	¾ cup	175 mL
Vanilla	1 tsp.	5 mL
Blueberries, fresh or frozen	1 cup	250 mL
All purpose flour	1 tbsp.	15 mL

In large bowl put flour, baking powder and salt. Stir together thoroughly. Make a well in center.

In another bowl cream butter and sugar. Beat in egg until quite smooth. Mix in milk and vanilla. Pour into well. Stir just to moisten. Batter will be lumpy.

Stir blueberries with flour lightly. Fold into batter. Fill greased muffin cups ¾ full. Bake in 400°F (200°C) oven for 25 minutes until nicely browned. Makes 16 muffins.

Pictured on page 17.

BLUEBERRY APPLE MUFFINS: Cut blueberries to ½ cup (125 mL). Add ½ cup (125 mL) diced, unpeeled apple. Add ½ tsp. (2 mL) cinnamon. Proceed as directed.

PLAIN MUFFINS: Omit blueberries. Sugar can be cut to 2 tbsp. (30 mL). Excellent served with Strawberry Butter.

NUTTY MUFFINS: Omit blueberries. Add ½ cup finely chopped hazelnuts, pecans or walnuts. Sprinkle 2 tbsp. (30 mL) nuts on top before baking.

BRAN MUFFINS

Can easily be doubled for freezing. Top notch. Gail's favorite.

All purpose flour	1 cup	250 mL
Baking powder	1 tsp.	5 mL
Baking soda	1 tsp.	5 mL
Salt	½ tsp.	2 mL
Raisins	¾ cup	175 mL
Buttermilk or sour milk	1 cup	250 mL
Natural bran	1 cup	250 mL
Cooking oil	⅓ cup	75 mL
Molasses	3 tbsp.	50 mL
Egg	1	1
Packed brown sugar	¼ cup	50 mL
Vanilla	½ tsp.	2 mL

In large bowl put flour, baking powder, soda, salt and raisins. Stir together well. Push up around sides of bowl making well in center.

In another bowl stir buttermilk with bran. Let stand 5 minutes.

Add remaining ingredients to bran mixture in order given. Beat with spoon until mixed. Pour into well in first bowl. Stir just to moisten. Batter will be lumpy. Fill greased muffin tins ¾ full. Bake in 375°F (190°C) oven for 20-25 minutes. Let stand 5 minutes. Remove from pan. Makes 12.

CARROT BRAN MUFFINS

The pineapple makes this muffin tender and very moist.

All purpose flour	1½ cups	375 mL
Packed brown sugar	¾ cup	175 mL
Natural bran	¾ cup	175 mL
Baking powder	1 tsp.	5 mL
Baking soda	1 tsp.	5 mL
Salt	½ tsp.	2 mL
Cinnamon	1 tsp.	5 mL
Eggs	2	2
Cooking oil	½ cup	125 mL
Grated carrot	1 cup	250 mL
Crushed pineapple and juice	1 cup	250 mL

(continued on next page)

Combine first seven ingredients in large bowl. Mix together. Make a well in center.

Beat eggs in mixing bowl until frothy. Mix in oil, carrots, pineapple and juice. Pour into well. Stir only to moisten. Batter will be lumpy. Fill greased muffin cups ¾ full. Bake in 400°F (200°C) oven for 20-25 minutes. Remove from pan after 5 minutes. Yield: 14 muffins.

CARROT MUFFINS: Omit bran. Change flour to 2 cups (500 mL).

COFFEE CAKE MUFFINS

These provide a taste of coffee cake in smaller servings.

All purpose flour	1½ cups	375 mL
Baking powder	2 tsp.	10 mL
Salt	½ tsp.	2 mL
Butter or margarine	¼ cup	50 mL
Granulated sugar	½ cup	125 mL
Egg	1	1
Milk	¾ cup	175 mL
Vanilla	½ tsp.	2 mL

Put flour, baking powder and salt in large bowl. Stir together. Make a well in center.

Beat butter, sugar and egg together well. Mix in milk and vanilla. Pour into well. Stir to moisten. Spoon part of batter into greased muffin tins ⅓ full. Sprinkle spice mix over top. Spoon rest of batter over top filling ⅔ full. Bake in 400°F (200°C) oven for 20 to 25 minutes. Yield: 12 muffins.

SPICE MIX

Packed brown sugar	½ cup	125 mL
All purpose flour	2 tbsp.	30 mL
Cinnamon	1 tsp.	5 mL

In small bowl combine all ingredients. Stir together well. Sprinkle it over batter as directed above.

Pictured on page 17.

...AN GRAHAM MUFFINS

Must be the "Cadillac" of Bran Muffins. Nutty texture, chock full of nutrition.

All bran cereal	1 cup	250 mL
Graham cracker crumbs	1 cup	250 mL
All purpose flour	½ cup	125 mL
Whole wheat or white flour	2 tbsp.	30 mL
Brown sugar, packed	¼ cup	50 mL
Wheat germ	¼ cup	50 mL
Baking soda	1 tsp.	5 mL
Salt	¼ tsp.	2 mL
Raisins, coarsely cut	½ cup	125 mL
Egg	1	1
Cooking oil	⅓ cup	75 mL
Molasses	¼ cup	50 mL
Buttermilk	¾ cup	175 mL
Vanilla	½ tsp.	2 mL

Measure all dry ingredients into bowl. Mix in raisins.

In another bowl beat egg until frothy. Add oil, molasses, buttermilk and vanilla. Beat to mix. Pour over dry ingredients. Stir just enough to moisten. Spoon into greased muffin tins, filling ¾ full. Bake in 375°F (190°C) oven for 20 minutes. Makes 12.

Pictured on cover.

1. Blueberry Muffins page 13
2. Banana Date Muffins page 12
3. Ginger Muffins page 26
4. Apple Streusel Muffins page 9
5. Cheese Bran Muffins page 20
6. Corn Muffins page 21
7. Coffee Cake Muffins page 15
8. Chocolate Filled Muffins page 19
9. Poppy Seed Muffins page 32
10. Banana Oatmeal Muffins page 12
11. Peanut Butter Muffins page 29
12. Banana Chip Muffins page 10
13. Date Muffins page 24
14. Six Week Muffins page 31

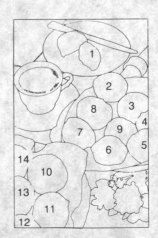

These showy muffins would do any tea table proud.

All purpose flour	2 cups	500 mL
Granulated sugar	¾ cup	175 mL
Cocoa	¼ cup	50 mL
Baking powder	3 tsp.	15 mL
Salt	½ tsp.	2 mL
Cinnamon	½ tsp.	2 mL
Egg	1	1
Milk	1 cup	250 mL
Cooking oil	⅓ cup	75 mL

FILLING:

Skim milk powder	¼ cup	50 mL
Hot water	2 tbsp.	35 mL
Butter or margarine	1 tsp.	5 mL
Almond flavoring	¼ tsp.	1 mL
Coconut, flake or medium	1 cup	250 mL

In large bowl put flour, sugar, cocoa, baking powder, salt and cinnamon. Stir together. Make well in center.

Beat eggs slightly. Stir in milk and oil. Pour into well. Stir to moisten. Fill greased muffin cups ¾ full.

In small bowl mix milk powder with hot water. Stir vigorously to blend well. Add butter and almond. Mix. Stir in coconut. Form into as many balls as muffins. Push into top center of each muffin. Bake in 400°F (200°C) oven for 20–25 minutes. Yield: 16 muffins.

Variation: Omit coconut balls. Use well drained maraschino cherries to push into muffins.

Pictured on page 17.

On your way through life don't worry if you stumble now and then. Only worms can't fall down.

CHEESE AND BACON MUFFINS

Breakfast on the run — coffee and a savory muffin.

All purpose flour	2 cups	500 mL
Granulated sugar	2 tbsp.	30 mL
Baking powder	1 tbsp.	15 mL
Salt	¼ tsp.	1 mL
Grated sharp cheddar cheese	½ cup	125 mL
Bacon slices, cooked and crumbled	4-5	4-5
Egg, slightly beaten	1	1
Milk	1 cup	250 mL
Cooking oil	¼ cup	50 mL

Measure first six dry ingredients into large bowl. Stir thoroughly. Make a well in center.

Beat egg slightly in small bowl. Mix in milk and oil. Pour into well. Stir only to moisten. Batter will be lumpy. Fill greased muffin cups ¾ full. Bake in 400°F (200°C) oven for 20-25 minutes. Let stand 5 minutes. Remove from pan. Serve warm. Makes 12.

Note: Exchange milk for 1 tin condensed cream of chicken or mushroom soup for another different savory muffin.

Pictured on page 125.

CHEESE BRAN MUFFINS

Just an excellent cheesey muffin.

All bran cereal	1 cup	250 mL
Buttermilk or sour milk	1¼ cups	300 mL
Egg	1	1
Cooking oil	¼ cup	50 mL
All purpose flour	1½ cups	375 mL
Granulated sugar	¼ cup	50 mL
Baking powder	1½ tsp.	7 mL
Baking soda	½ tsp.	2 mL
Salt	½ tsp.	2 mL
Grated sharp cheddar cheese	1 cup	250 mL

(continued on next page)

Combine cereal and buttermilk in small bowl.

In medium bowl beat egg until frothy. Stir in oil and cereal mixture.

In large bowl combine all remaining ingredients. Make a well in center.

Pour batter into well. Stir only to moisten. Batter will be lumpy. Fill greased muffin cups ¾ full. Bake in 400°F (200°C) oven for 20-25 minutes. Let stand 5 minutes. Remove from pan. Serve warm. Makes 16.

Pictured on page 17.

CORN MUFFINS

Not sweet tasting. Good for lunch or in place of dinner rolls for a different touch.

All purpose flour	1¼ cups	300 mL
Corn meal	1 cup	250 mL
Granulated sugar	¼ cup	50 mL
Baking powder	4 tsp.	20 mL
Salt	½ tsp.	2 mL
Egg	1	1
Cooking oil	¼ cup	50 mL
Milk	1 cup	250 mL

Measure flour, meal, sugar, baking powder and salt into large bowl. Stir together. Make well in the center

Beat egg in small bowl until frothy. Mix in oil and milk. Pour into well. Stir just enough to moisten. Batter will be lumpy. Fill greased muffin cups ¾ full. Bake in 400°F (200°C) oven for 20-25 minutes. Leave in pan 5 minutes, then remove. Serve warm. Makes 15.

Pictured on page 17.

CARROT SPICE MUFFINS

Dark and nutritious with spicy overtones.

All purpose flour	1½ cups	375 mL
Natural bran	1½ cups	375 mL
Wheat germ	¼ cup	50 mL
Packed brown sugar	½ cup	125 mL
Baking soda	2 tsp.	10 mL
Salt	½ tsp.	2 mL
Cinnamon	1 tsp.	5 mL
Nutmeg	¼ tsp.	1 mL
Eggs	2	2
Molasses	¼ cup	50 mL
Cooking oil	¼ cup	50 mL
Milk	1½ cups	375 mL
Vinegar	2 tbsp.	60 mL
Grated carrot	1 cup	250 mL
Chopped walnuts	½ cup	125 mL
Chopped dates or raisins	1 cup	250 mL

Combine first eight dry ingredients in large bowl. Make a well in the center.

Beat eggs in separate bowl. Add all remaining ingredients and stir to mix. Pour into well. Stir just enough to moisten. Fill greased muffin cups ¾ full. Bake in 400°F (200°C) oven for 20-25 minutes. Makes 36.

Pictured on page 125.

If you build a huge castle with no bath tubs, you will be known as filthy rich.

The sugared topping finishes these off nicely.

All purpose flour	2 cups	500 mL
Granulated sugar	½ cup	125 mL
Baking powder	4 tsp.	20 mL
Salt	½ tsp.	2 mL
Eggs	2	2
Cooking oil	¼ cup	50 mL
Milk	½ cup	125 mL
Whole cranberry sauce	1 cup	250 mL

Measure flour, sugar, baking powder and salt into large bowl. Stir thoroughly. Make a well in center.

In separate bowl beat eggs until frothy. Mix in oil, milk and cranberries. Pour into well. Stir to moisten. Batter will be lumpy. Fill muffin tins ¾ full. Bake in 400°F (200°C) oven for 20-25 minutes. Makes 18-24 muffins.

TOPPING: Brush hot cooked muffin tops with melted butter. Sprinkle with granulated sugar.

FRESH CRANBERRY MUFFINS: Use coarsely chopped or whole cranberries instead of cranberry sauce. Add a bit more milk just so batter is not too stiff to spoon out.

Don't buy a turkey that is missing a leg or a wing. Buy the complete bird — it won the fight!

DATE MUFFINS

Full of dates. Moist and yummy.

Chopped dates	1½ cups	375 mL
Boiling water	¾ cup	175 mL
Baking soda	1 tsp.	5 mL
All purpose flour	1¾ cups	425 mL
Baking powder	1 tsp.	5 mL
Salt	½ tsp.	2 mL
Chopped walnuts	½ cup	125 mL
Eggs	2	2
Packed brown sugar	¾ cup	175 mL
Cooking oil	¼ cup	50 mL
Vanilla	1 tsp.	5 mL

Combine dates, water and soda in bowl. Set aside.

In second bowl put flour, baking powder, salt and nuts. Stir well. Set aside.

In mixing bowl beat eggs until frothy. Slowly blend in sugar, oil and vanilla. Stir in date mixture. Pour in dry ingredients from second bowl. Stir just to combine. Don't worry if the batter is lumpy. Fill greased muffin tins ¾ full. Bake in 400°F (200°C) oven for 20-25 minutes. Remove from pan after 5 minutes. Yield: 16 muffins.

Pictured on page 17.

FRUIT MUFFINS

A very moist muffin. Uses leftover fruit.

All purpose flour	2 cups	500 mL
Baking powder	1 tsp.	5 mL
Baking soda	1 tsp.	5 mL
Salt	1 tsp.	5 mL
Butter or margarine	½ cup	125 mL
Granulated sugar	½ cup	125 mL
Egg	1	1
Milk	1 cup	250 mL
Diced canned fruit, drained	¾ cup	175 mL

(continued on next page)

In large bowl mix together flour, baking powder, soda and salt. Make a well in the center.

Using a smaller bowl, cream butter, sugar and egg together well. Mix in milk and fruit. Pour into well. Stir just to moisten. Batter will be lumpy. Fill greased muffin cups ¾ full. Bake in 400°F (200°C) oven for 20-25 minutes. Leave in pan 5 minutes, then remove. Serve warm. Makes 16.

FRUITED MUFFINS

Spicy and colorful.

All purpose flour	2 cups	500 mL
Baking powder	1 tsp.	5 mL
Baking soda	1 tsp.	5 mL
Salt	¾ tsp.	5 mL
Cinnamon	1 tsp.	5 mL
Raisins	½ cup	125 mL
Glazed mixed fruit	½ cup	125 mL
Butter or margarine	½ cup	125 mL
Granulated sugar	¾ cup	175 mL
Egg	1	1
Buttermilk	1 cup	250 mL
Vanilla	½ tsp.	2 mL

Measure first seven dry ingredients into large bowl. Mix together. Make a well in the center.

Cream butter, sugar and egg together well in smaller bowl. Mix in buttermilk and vanilla. Pour into well. Stir just enough to moisten. Batter will be lumpy. Fill greased muffin cups ¾ full. Bake in 400°F (200°C) oven for 20-25 minutes. Wait 5 minutes for easier removal of muffins. Serve warm. Makes 18.

VANILLA GLAZE: Mix enough water or milk with ¾ cup (175 mL) icing sugar to make a runny glaze. Drizzle over muffins.

GINGER MUFFINS

Dark and different, a lunchbox surprise. Better double this recipe.

Butter or margarine	¼ cup	50 mL
Granulated sugar	¼ cup	50 mL
Egg	1	1
Molasses	½ cup	125 mL
Hot water	¼ cup	50 mL
All purpose flour	1¾ cups	425 mL
Baking soda	1 tsp.	5 mL
Salt	¼ tsp.	1 mL
Cinnamon	½ tsp.	3 mL
Ginger	½ tsp.	2 mL
Cloves	¼ tsp.	1 mL
Hot water	¼ cup	50 mL

Combine butter, sugar, egg, molasses and first amount of hot water in mixing bowl. Beat together well.

Measure next six dry ingredients into same bowl. Stir together.

Gradually stir hot water into batter. Fill greased muffin tins ¾ full. Bake in 400°F (200°C) oven for 20-25 minutes until inserted toothpick comes out clean. Cool in pan 5 minutes, then remove. Makes 12 muffins.

Pictured on page 17.

MINCEMEAT MUFFINS

Nutritious and delicious.

All purpose flour	1 cup	250 mL
Whole wheat flour	1 cup	250 mL
Granulated sugar	¼ cup	50 mL
Baking powder	1 tsp.	5 mL
Baking soda	1 tsp.	5 mL
Salt	½ tsp.	2 mL
Cinnamon	½ tsp.	2 mL
Egg	1	1
Cooking oil	¼ cup	50 mL
Mincement	1 cup	250 mL
Milk or fruit juice	½ cup	125 mL

(continued on next page)

Measure all seven dry ingredients into large bowl. Stir together. Make a well in the center.

In another bowl beat egg until frothy. Mix in oil, mincemeat and milk. Pour into well. Stir only to moisten. Batter will be lumpy. Fill greased muffin cups ¾ full. Bake in 400°F (200°C) oven for 20-25 minutes. Let stand 5 minutes. Remove from pan. Serve warm. Makes 18.

Pictured on cover.

OATMEAL MUFFINS

A good rich flavor.

All purpose flour	1¼ cups	300 mL
Rolled oats	1 cup	250 mL
Packed brown sugar	¼ cup	50 mL
Baking powder	3 tsp.	15 mL
Salt	½ tsp.	2 mL
Cinnamon	¼ tsp.	2 mL
Raisins	¾ cup	175 mL
Egg	1	1
Molasses	2 tbsp.	30 mL
Cooking oil	¼ cup	50 mL
Milk	1 cup	250 mL
Vanilla	1 tsp.	5 mL

Measure all first seven dry ingredients into large bowl. Mix together. Make a well in the center.

Beat egg in small bowl until frothy. Mix in molasses, oil, milk and vanilla. Pour into well. Stir only to moisten. Batter will be lumpy. Fill greased muffin cups ¾ full. Bake in 400°F (200°C) oven for 20 to 25 minutes. Let stand 5 minutes. Remove from pan. Serve warm. Makes 16.

ORANGE MUFFINS

A delicious orange flavor with little date flecks throughout. Scrumptious!

Orange with peel, cut up	1	1
Orange juice	½ cup	125 mL
Chopped dates	½ cup	125 mL
Egg	1	1
Butter or margarine	½ cup	125 mL
All purpose flour	1¾ cups	425 mL
Granulated sugar	¾ cup	175 mL
Baking powder	1 tsp.	5 mL
Baking soda	1 tsp.	5 mL

Cut orange into 7 or 8 pieces. Remove seeds. Combine orange pieces and juice in blender. Puree. Add dates, egg and butter to blender. Blend. Pour into medium size bowl.

Measure flour, sugar, baking powder and soda in separate bowl. Mix thoroughly. Pour over top of orange mixture. Stir to combine. Fill greased muffin tins ¾ full. Bake in 400°F (200°C) oven for 20 minutes. Remove from pans after 5 minutes standing time. Make 12 large or 16 medium muffins.

Pictured on cover.

ORANGE BRAN MUFFINS

The orange gives a real tang. A super muffin.

All purpose flour	1 cup	250 mL
All bran cereal or bran	1 cup	250 mL
Baking powder	1 tsp.	5 mL
Baking soda	1 tsp.	5 mL
Salt	¼ tsp.	1 mL
Packed brown sugar	½ cup	125 mL
Nutmeg	⅛ tsp.	1 mL
Egg	1	1
Cooking oil	¼ cup	50 mL
Sour milk or butter milk	¾ cup	175 mL
Orange juice	2 tbsp.	30 mL
Orange rind	1 tsp.	5 mL
Chopped dates	1 cup	250 mL

(continued on next page)

Measure first seven dry ingredients into mixing bowl. Stir thoroughly to blend. Make a well in center.

In another bowl beat egg until frothy. Mix in oil, sour milk, orange juice, rind and dates. Pour into well. Stir just enough to moisten. Batter will be lumpy. Fill greased muffin cups ¾ full. Bake in 400°F (200°C) oven for 20-25 minutes. Yield: 12 muffins.

Note: To make sour milk add milk to 1 tbsp. (15 mL) vinegar to measure ¾ cup (175 mL).

PEANUT BUTTER MUFFINS

Nutrition packed in a small package.

All purpose flour	1½ cups	375 mL
Granulated sugar	¼ cup	50 mL
Baking powder	3 tsp.	15 mL
Salt	½ tsp.	2 mL
All bran cereal	1 cup	250 mL
Milk	1 cup	250 mL
Egg	1	1
Peanut butter	½ cup	125 mL
Cooking oil	¼ cup	50 mL
Milk	¼ cup	50 mL

Put flour, sugar, baking powder and salt into large bowl. Stir to mix. Make a well in the center.

Combine cereal with milk in medium bowl.

Add egg and peanut butter to cereal. Beat with spoon to mix well. Add oil and milk. Stir. Pour into well. Stir just enough to moisten. Batter will be lumpy. Fill greased muffin cups ¾ full. Bake in 400°F (200°C) oven for 20-25 minutes. Wait 5 minutes for easier removal of muffins. Serve warm. Makes 16.

Pictured on page 17.

RAISIN MUFFINS

Good rich color loaded with raisins.

Raisins	1½ cups	375 mL
Water	1 cup	250 mL
Butter or margarine	½ cup	125 mL
Packed brown sugar	¾ cup	175 mL
Egg	1	1
Vanilla	1 tsp.	5 mL
Raisin water	½ cup	125 mL
All purpose flour	2 cups	500 mL
Baking powder	1 tsp.	5 mL
Baking soda	1 tsp.	5 mL
Salt	¼ tsp.	2 mL
Cinnamon	½ tsp.	3 mL
Nutmeg	½ tsp.	2 mL

Put raisins and water in sauce pan. Bring to boil. Simmer covered 10 minutes until plump and tender. Remove from heat. Remove cover. Cool.

Cream butter, sugar and egg. Add vanilla. Drain raisins, measuring out ½ cup of juice. Stir raisins into batter.

Measure all remaining dry ingredients into separate large bowl. Stir to mix together. Add to batter alternately with raisin water stirring after each addition until barely blended. Fill greased muffin tins ¾ full. Bake in 375°F (190°C) oven for about 20 minutes. Serve warm. Yield: 18 muffins.

Note: Chopped nuts are a welcome addition.

SIX WEEK BRAN MUFFINS

Store batter in refrigerator. Bake a fresh supply every day if you like.

Bran flakes cereal	4 cups	1 L
All bran cereal	2 cups	500 mL
Boiling water	2 cups	500 mL
Butter or margarine	1 cup	250 mL
Granulated sugar	1½ cups	375 mL
Packed brown sugar	1½ cups	375 mL
Eggs	4	4
Buttermilk	4 cups	1 L
Molasses (optional)	¼ cup	50 mL
All purpose flour	5 cups	1.25 L
Baking soda	2 tbsp.	30 mL
Baking powder	1 tbsp.	15 mL
Salt	1 tsp.	5 mL
Raisins	2 cups	500 mL

In large bowl put cereals and boiling water. Let stand.

In mixing bowl cream butter and sugars together. Beat in eggs one at a time beating well after each addition. Mix in buttermilk. Add molasses. Stir in cereal mixture.

In another bowl put flour, soda, baking powder, salt and raisins. Mix thoroughly. Add to batter. Stir to combine. Store in refrigerator. It will keep for six weeks. As required, fill greased muffin cups ¾ full. Bake in 400°F (200°C) oven for 20-25 minutes. Remove from pan after 5 minutes.

Variation: Brans may be switched to use 2 cups (500 mL) bran flakes and 4 cups (1 L) all bran cereal. Or you may use natural bran to replace one cereal.

Pictured on page 17.

PINEAPPLE MUFFINS

A delicately flavored fine textured muffin.

All purpose flour	2 cups	500 mL
Granulated sugar	½ cup	125 mL
Baking powder	3 tsp.	15 mL
Salt	½ tsp.	2 mL
Egg	1	1
Cooking oil	¼ cup	50 mL
Milk	1 cup	250 mL
Well drained crushed pineapple	½ cup	125 mL

Measure flour, sugar, baking powder and salt in large bowl. Stir. Make a well in center.

Beat egg in small bowl until frothy. Mix in oil, milk and pineapple. Pour into well. Stir just enough to moisten. Batter will be lumpy. Fill greased muffin cups ¾ full. Bake in 400°F (200°C) oven for 20-25 minutes. Wait 5 minutes for easier removal of muffins. Serve warm. Makes 18.

POPPY SEED MUFFINS

Serve warm with maple butter for the best treat going.

Milk	1 cup	250 mL
Poppy seeds	½ cup	125 mL
Butter or margarine	¼ cup	50 mL
Granulated sugar	3 tbsp.	50 mL
Egg	1	1
Vanilla	1 tsp.	5 mL
All purpose flour	2 cups	500 mL
Baking powder	3 tsp.	15 mL
Salt	¾ tsp.	5 mL

(continued on next page)

Put milk and poppy seeds into small bowl. Let stand for 10 minutes or so.

Cream butter, sugar and egg together well. Add vanilla. Stir in poppy seed mixture.

Measure flour, baking powder and salt into large bowl. Stir to mix thoroughly. Make well in center. Pour wet mixture in well. Stir only to moisten. Fill greased muffin tins ¾ full. Bake in 400°F (200°C) oven for 20 to 25 minutes. Serve warm. Makes 15.

Pictured on page 17.

ZUCCHINI MUFFINS

Ever popular. Good and spicy with whole wheat flour as an extra benefit.

All purpose flour	1 cup	250 mL
Whole wheat flour	1 cup	250 mL
Baking powder	1½ tsp.	7 mL
Baking soda	½ tsp.	2 mL
Cinnamon	1 tsp.	5 mL
Allspice	½ tsp.	2 mL
Salt	1 tsp.	5 mL
Egg	1	1
Cooking oil	¼ cup	50 mL
Granulated sugar	½ cup	125 mL
Grated zucchini	1 cup	250 mL
Milk	½ cup	125 mL

Measure into large bowl all seven dry ingredients. Stir thoroughly. Make a well in the center.

Beat egg in smaller bowl until frothy. Mix in oil, sugar, zucchini and milk. Pour into well. Stir only to moisten. Batter will be lumpy. Fill greased muffin cups ¾ full. Bake in 400°F (200°C) oven for 20-25 minutes. Let stand 5 minutes. Remove from pan. Serve warm. Makes 12 large muffins.

Pictured on cover.

PUMPKIN MUFFINS

Moist and tender. A delicious muffin.

All purpose flour	1½ cups	375 mL
Baking powder	1 tsp.	5 mL
Baking soda	1 tsp.	5 mL
Salt	½ tsp.	2 mL
Cinnamon	½ tsp.	3 mL
Nutmeg	½ tsp.	2 mL
Ginger	½ tsp.	2 mL
Raisins	½ cup	125 mL
Egg	1	1
Granulated sugar	¼ cup	50 mL
Cooking oil	⅓ cup	75 mL
Cooked pumpkin	1 cup	250 mL
Milk	¼ cup	60 mL

Combine all first eight dry ingredients in large bowl. Stir thoroughly. Make a well in the center.

Beat egg in small bowl until frothy. Mix in sugar, oil, pumpkin and milk. Pour into well. Stir only to moisten. Batter will be lumpy. Fill greased muffin cups ¾ full. Bake in 400°F (200°C) oven for 20–25 minutes. Let stand 5 minutes. Remove from pan. Serve warm. Makes 14.

ORANGE PUMPKIN MUFFINS: Add 1½ tbsp. (25 mL) grated orange rind to batter.

1. Apricot Raisin Loaf page 39
2. Favorite Nut page 57
3. Cherry Spice Loaf page 45
4. Cinnamon Coconut Loaf page 47
5. Chocolate Chip Date Loaf page 43
6. Orange Loaf page 66
7. Merry Fruit Bread page 63
8. Apricot Cheese Loaf page 40
9. Date Graham Loaf page 56
10. Cranberry Banana Loaf page 52
11. Fruit Bread page 58
12. Barm Brack page 42
13. Poppy Seed Loaf page 69

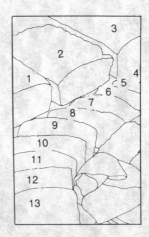

WHOLE WHEAT MUF

Can you believe nutrition tasting so good?

Whole wheat flour	2 cups	500 mL
Granulated sugar	¼ cup	50 mL
Baking powder	3 tsp.	15 mL
Salt	½ tsp.	2 mL
Beaten egg	1	1
Milk	1 cup	250 mL
Cooking oil	¼ cup	50 mL

Stir flour, sugar, baking powder and salt together in bowl. Make a well in the center.

Pour in egg, milk and oil in the well. Stir just to moisten. Fill greased muffin tins ¾ full. Bake in 400°F (200°C) oven for 20-25 minutes. Serve warm. Makes 12.

SPICED APPLE MUFFINS

First class spicy muffin. Good apple flavor.

All purpose flour	2 cups	500 mL
Bran flakes	1 cup	250 mL
Packed brown sugar	⅔ cup	150 mL
Baking powder	3 tsp.	15 mL
Salt	1 tsp.	5 mL
Cinnamon	½ tsp.	2 mL
Nutmeg	¼ tsp.	2 mL
Eggs	2	2
Milk	⅔ cup	150 mL
Cooking oil	¼ cup	50 mL
Grated peeled apple	1 cup	250 mL

In mixing bowl, put flour, bran flakes, sugar, baking powder, salt and spices. Fluff together with a fork to thoroughly distribute baking powder. Pushing mixture up sides of bowl, make a well in center.

In medium bowl beat eggs slightly. Stir in milk, oil and apple. Stir together. Pour into well. Quickly stir to moisten. Batter will be lumpy. Spoon into greased muffin pans. Bake in 400°F (200°C) oven for 15-20 minutes. Yield: 16 muffins.

Pictured on cover.

APPLE LOAF

A tender loaf with a delicate apple flavor.

Butter or margarine	½ cup	125 mL
Granulated sugar	1 cup	250 mL
Eggs	2	2
Vanilla	1 tsp.	5 mL
Coarsely shredded, unpeeled apple, packed	1 cup	250 mL
All purpose flour	2 cups	500 mL
Baking Powder	1 tsp.	5 mL
Baking soda	½ tsp.	2 mL
Salt	½ tsp.	2 mL
Chopped walnuts	½ cup	125 mL

Put butter, sugar and 1 egg in bowl. Beat until smooth. Add second egg and beat well. Stir in vanilla.

Shred apple on a fairly coarse grater. Stir in.

Mix flour, baking powder, soda, salt and nuts together in another bowl. Pour into batter. Stir only until moistened. Scrape into greased 9 × 5 × 3 inch (23 × 12 × 7 cm) loaf pan. Bake in 350°F (180°C) oven for 50-60 minutes until an inserted toothpick comes out clean. Let stand 10 minutes then remove from pan. Place on a rack to cool. Wrap. Yield: 1 loaf.

A kid's idea of a balanced diet is a hamburger in each hand.

A super loaf, flavorful and fruity.

Butter or margarine	¼ cup	50mL
Packed brown sugar	¾ cup	175 mL
Eggs	2	2
Orange juice	1 cup	250 mL
All purpose flour	2 cups	500 mL
Baking powder	2 tsp.	10 mL
Salt	1 tsp.	5 mL
Dried apricots, coarsely chopped	1 cup	250 mL
Raisins	1 cup	250 mL
Chopped pecans or walnuts	½ cup	125 mL
Finely grated orange rind	1 tbsp.	15 mL

Beat butter, sugar and 1 egg together until smooth. Beat in second egg. Blend in orange juice.

Using a second bowl measure in flour, baking powder and salt. Stir in apricots, raisins, nuts and rind. Pour all at once over batter in first bowl. Stir just to moisten. Scrape into greased loaf pan 9 × 5 × 3 inch (23 × 12 × 7 cm). Bake in 350°F (180°C) oven for 1 hour until it tests done. Let stand 10 minutes. Remove from pan and place on rack to cool. Wrap. Make a day or two ahead for easy cutting and better flavour. Yield: 1 loaf.

Glaze: Heat together 3 tbsp. (50 mL) apricot jam and 1 tbsp. (15 mL) water. Put through strainer. Spoon over hot loaf.

Pictured on page 35.

Don't let your dog eat garlic or his bark really will be worse than his bite.

BANANA BREAD

An old stand-by. Quite dark with lots of flecks.

Butter or margarine	½ cup	125 mL
Granulated sugar	1 cup	250 mL
Eggs	2	2
Mashed very ripe bananas (3 medium)	1 cup	250 mL
All purpose flour	2 cups	500 mL
Baking soda	1 tsp.	5 mL
Baking powder	½ tsp.	2 mL
Salt	½ tsp.	2 mL
Chopped walnuts	1 cup	250 mL

Cream butter and sugar together. Beat in eggs one at a time, beating until smooth. Add mashed bananas and blend in.

In second bowl, stir flour with baking soda, baking powder, salt and nuts. Add to banana mixture stirring only to moisten. Transfer to greased 9 × 5 × 3 inch (23 × 12 × 7 cm) loaf pan. Bake in 350°F (180°C) oven for about 1 hour until inserted toothpick comes out clean. Let stand 10 minutes. Remove from pan and place on cake rack to cool. Wrap to store. Yield: 1 loaf.

BANANA CHIP BREAD: Add ¾ cup (175 mL) semi-sweet chocolate chips.

APRICOT CHEESE LOAF

A showy loaf, a bit tart.

Boiling water	1 cup	250 mL
Cut up dried apricots	1 cup	250 mL
Butter or margarine	3 tbsp.	50 mL
Small package of cream cheese	½ cup	125 mL
Granulated sugar	1 cup	250 mL
Eggs	2	2
All purpose flour	2 cups	500 mL
Baking powder	2 tsp.	10 mL
Baking soda	½ tsp.	2 mL
Salt	½ tsp.	2 mL
Dates, cut up	1 cup	250 mL

(continued on next page)

Pour boiling water over apricot pieces in small bowl. Cool.

Cream butter and softened cheese with sugar. Beat in eggs one at a time until smooth. Stir in cooled apricots and water.

In another bowl combine flour, baking powder, soda, salt and dates. Mix well. Pour into batter and stir until moisted. Turn into greased 9 × 5 × 3 inch (23 × 12 × 7 cm) loaf pan. Bake in 350°F (180°C) oven for 1 hour until it tests done. Let stand 10 minutes. Remove from pan to rack. Cool and wrap. Yield: 1 loaf.

Pictured on page 35.

━━━ BANANA COCONUT LOAF ━━━

Pretty as a picture with flavor to match.

Eggs	2	2
Granulated sugar	1 cup	250 mL
Butter or margarine, melted	½ cup	125 mL
Mashed ripe bananas (3 medium)	1 cup	250 mL
Almond flavoring	½ tsp.	2 mL
All purpose flour	1½ cups	375 mL
Medium grind coconut	½ cup	125 mL
Baking powder	1½ tsp.	7 mL
Baking soda	½ tsp.	2 mL
Salt	½ tsp.	2 mL
Chopped walnuts	½ oup	125 mL
Maraschino cherries cut up	½ cup	125 mL

Break eggs in mixing bowl. Beat until light and frothy. Add sugar and melted butter. Beat well. Stir in mashed banana and flavoring.

In another bowl, measure in remaining ingredients. Stir until well mixed. Pour over batter. Stir just to combine. Spoon into greased loaf pan 9 × 5 × 3 inches (23 × 12 × 7 cm). Bake for 1 hour in 350°F (180°C) oven until toothpick inserted in center comes out clean. Let stand for 10 minutes. Remove from pan. Cool. Wrap. Yield: 1 loaf.

Pictured on cover.

BARM BRACK

To make this Irish loaf, it must be planned the previous evening. You will find this a moist, different loaf. Good.

Cold leftover tea	1 cup	250 mL
Raisins	1 cup	250 mL
Peel	½ cup	125 mL
Currants	½ cup	125 mL
Granulated sugar	1 cup	250 mL
Egg	1	1
Melted butter or margarine	¼ cup	50 mL
All purpose flour	2 cups	500 mL
Baking powder	1 tsp.	7 mL
Baking soda	¼ tsp.	2 mL
Salt	¼ tsp.	1 mL

Put tea in a large bowl along with raisins, peel, currants and sugar. Let stand covered overnight.

Next morning beat egg until frothy. Stir into fruit mixture. Stir melted butter into fruit.

Combine and stir the four remaining dry ingredients. Add to fruit batter. Stir until blended. Spoon into greased loaf pan 9 × 5 × 3 inch (23 × 12 × 7 cm). Bake in 350°F (180°C) oven for 60-70 minutes. Cool 10 minutes. Turn out on rack to cool. Serve sliced with butter. Yield: 1 loaf.

Pictured on page 35.

Think of it — you can walk a mile and yet only move two feet.

CHOCOLATE CHIP DATE LOAF

Dark and delicious with a fine texture. A large loaf. Good! Good!

Chopped dates	1 cup	250 mL
Baking soda	1 tsp.	5 mL
Boiling water	1 cup	250 mL
Vanilla	1 tsp.	5 mL
Butter or margarine	¾ cup	175 mL
Granulated sugar	1 cup	250 mL
Eggs	2	2
All purpose flour	2 cups	500 mL
Cocoa	½ cup	125 mL
Baking soda	1 tsp.	5 mL
Salt	½ tsp.	2 mL
Semi-sweet chocolate chips	½ cup	125 mL

In a small bowl combine dates, soda, boiling water and vanilla. Stir. Set aside to cool a little.

In mixing bowl cream butter and sugar. Beat eggs in one at a time, beating until smooth. Add date mixture. Stir.

Measure flour, cocoa, soda, salt and chips into a separate bowl. Stir to mix well then pour flour mixture in mixing bowl. Blend until just moistened. Spoon into greased 9 × 5 × 3 inch (23 × 12 × 7 cm) loaf pan. Bake for 1 hour in 350°F (180°C) oven or until it tests done. Wait about 10 minutes for loaf to cool a bit before removing it to a rack to finish cooling. Wrap. Yield: 1 loaf.

Pictured on page 35.

Those two like to argue so much that they won't even eat anything that agrees with them.

CARROT LOAF

Really tasty and spicy.

Cooking oil	½ cup	125 mL
Eggs	2	2
Granulated sugar	1 cup	250 mL
Finely grated carrots	1 cup	250 mL
All purpose flour	1¾ cups	425 mL
Baking powder	2 tsp.	10 mL
Baking soda	½ tsp.	2 mL
Cinnamon	1 tsp.	5 mL
Nutmeg	¾ tsp.	4 mL
Cloves	¼ tsp.	1 mL
Ginger	¼ tsp.	1 mL
Chopped walnuts	½ cup	125 mL

Beat oil, eggs and sugar together until blended. Stir in carrots.

In another bowl mix all remaining ingredients to combine. Pour into carrot batter. Stir only to moisten. Turn into greased 9 × 5 × 3 (23 × 12 × 7 cm) loaf pan. Bake in 350°F (180°C) oven for about 1 hour or until an inserted toothpick comes out clean. Allow to stand for 10 minutes before removing from pan to cool on rack. Store in plastic bag. Yield: 1 loaf.

CHERRY MARASCHINO LOAF

The slices are flavored with color as well as taste. Pretty and pink.

Butter or margarine	¼ cup	50 mL
Granulated sugar	1 cup	250 mL
Egg	1	1
Milk	⅔ cup	150 mL
Maraschino cherry juice	⅓ cup	75 mL
Almond flavoring	1 tsp.	5 mL
All purpose flour	2 cups	500 mL
Baking powder	2 tsp.	10 mL
Salt	¼ tsp.	2 mL
Chopped walnuts	½ cup	125 mL
Chopped maraschino cherries	½-⅔ cup	75 mL

(continued on next page)

Put butter, sugar and egg in mixing bowl. Beat until smooth. Add milk, juice and flavoring.

In a separate bowl combine flour, baking powder and salt. Stir in nuts and cherries. Pour into batter. Moisten all ingredients by stirring as little as possible. Spoon into greased loaf pan 9 × 5 × 3 inch (23 × 12 × 7 cm). Bake in 350°F (180°C) oven. Test for doneness 45 minutes onward. Let stand 10 minutes. Turn loaf out onto rack to cool. Store in plastic bag. Yield: 1 loaf.

CHERRY SPICE LOAF

Looks pretty when sliced. Tastes good.

Eggs	2	2
Granulated sugar	1 cup	250 mL
Cooking oil	½ cup	125 mL
Milk	¾ cup	175 mL
Almond flavoring	½ tsp.	2 mL
All purpose flour	2 cups	500 mL
Baking powder	1½ tsp.	10 mL
Baking soda	½ tsp.	2 mL
Salt	¼ tsp.	2 mL
Dates, cut up	½ cup	125 mL
Glazed cherries	½ cup	125 mL
Raisins	½ cup	125 mL
Chopped walnuts	½ cup	125 mL

Beat eggs slightly. Beat in sugar and oil. Slowly add milk and almond.

In second bowl put flour, baking powder, soda and salt. Stir in dates, cherries, raisins and nuts. Pour into batter stirring only to moisten. Spoon into greased loaf pan 9 × 5 × 3 inch (23 × 12 × 7 cm). Bake for 1 hour in 350°F (180°C) oven until a toothpick inserted in the center comes out clean. After 10 minutes turn loaf out to cool on a rack. Store in plastic bag. Yield: 1 loaf.

Pictured on page 35.

CHOCOLATE DATE LOAF

A delicious tea bread. Serve with a spread.

Chopped dates	1 cup	250 mL
Boiling water	¾ cup	175 mL
Baking soda	1 tsp.	5 mL
Egg, beaten	1	1
Granulated sugar	½ cup	125 mL
Salt	¾ tsp.	5 mL
Vanilla	1 tsp.	5 mL
Semi-sweet chocolate chips, melted	¾ cup	175 mL
Butter or margarine, melted	¼ cup	50 mL
All purpose flour	1¾ cups	425 mL
Baking powder	1 tsp.	5 mL
Chopped walnuts	½ cup	125 mL

Combine chopped dates with boiling water and soda. Stir and allow to cool.

In mixing bowl beat egg lightly. Beat in sugar, salt and vanilla. In small saucepan melt chips and butter over low heat, stirring. Mix into batter. Stir in date mixture.

Put flour, baking powder and nuts into bowl. Stir together well. Add to batter. Stir to mix. Scrape into greased 9 × 5 × 3 inch (23 × 12 × 7 cm) loaf pan. Let stand 20 minutes. Bake in 350°F (180°C) oven for 1 hour or until it tests done. Cool in pan 10 minutes. Remove from pan. Cuts better second day. Yield: 1 loaf.

CINNAMON COCONUT LOAF

Scrumptious with a pretty swirl effect when sliced.

Eggs	2	2
Cooking oil	¼ cup	50 mL
Granulated sugar	1 cup	250 mL
Commercial sour cream	1 cup	250 mL
All purpose flour	1½ cups	375 mL
Baking powder	1½ tsp.	7 mL
Baking soda	1 tsp.	5 mL
Salt	¼ tsp.	1 mL
Coconut, medium grind	½ cup	125 mL
Packed brown sugar	¼ cup	50 mL
Cinnamon	2 tsp.	10 mL

In mixing bowl beat eggs until frothy. Beat in oil and sugar. Blend in sour cream.

In another bowl measure flour, baking powder, soda and salt. Mix well and add to first bowl. Stir until combined.

In small bowl stir coconut, brown sugar and cinnamon. Put ½ of the batter in the bottom of a greased 9 × 5 × 3 inch (23 × 12 × 7 cm) loaf pan. Sprinkle ½ cinnamon mixture over. Spread second half of batter over by putting dabs here and there. Sprinkle second half cinnamon mixture over top. Cut through batter with knife to give swirling, marbled effect. Bake in 350°F (180°C) oven for 1 hour. After loaf stands for 10 minutes, remove from pan to cool on rack. Wrap. Yield: 1 loaf.

Pictured on page 35.

Paré Pointer

She must be a weight lifter. She has raised so many dumbells.

COCONUT BREAD

A nice moist loaf for coconut lovers.

Butter or margarine	½ cup	125 mL
Granulated sugar	1 cup	250 mL
Eggs	2	2
Milk	½ cup	125 mL
Vanilla	1 tsp.	5 mL
All purpose flour	1½ cups	375 mL
Baking powder	1 tsp.	5 mL
Salt	½ tsp.	2 mL
Fine grind coconut	1 cup	250 mL

Cream butter and sugar together in mixing bowl. Beat in eggs one at a time. Mix in milk and vanilla.

In small bowl mix flour, baking powder, salt and coconut. Add to batter. Stir until blended. Scrape into greased 9 × 5 × 3 inch (23 × 12 × 7 cm) loaf pan. Bake in 350°F (180°C) oven for 60-70 minutes until an inserted toothpick comes out clean. Cool in pan 10 minutes. Remove to rack to finish cooling. Wrap to store. Yield: 1 loaf.

COTTAGE CHEESE LOAF

Very good served with salads, fruit, luncheon. Also a good way to use up the last of the cottage cheese. The flavor boost comes from the peel.

Cottage cheese	1 cup	250 mL
Packed brown sugar	1 cup	250 mL
Eggs	3	3
All purpose flour	1¾ cups	425 mL
Baking powder	2 tsp.	10 mL
Baking soda	½ tsp.	3 mL
Salt	½ tsp.	2 mL
Chopped walnuts	½ cup	125 mL
Chopped mixed peel	½ cup	125 mL

(continued on next page)

Smooth cottage cheese in a blender or force through strainer. Put into bowl. Beat in sugar. Add eggs one at a time beating well after each addition. Set aside.

Measure remaining ingredients into a second bowl. Mix together well. Pour into first bowl. Stir to moisten. Scrape into greased 9 × 5 × 3 inch (23 × 12 × 7 cm) loaf pan. Bake in 350°F (180°C) oven for about 1 hour. Cool for 10 minutes before turning out to finish cooling on rack. Wrap well. Serve with butter. Yield 1 loaf.

CRANBERRY LOAF

Almost tangy, you will wish this small loaf was huge.

All purpose flour	1 cup	250 mL
Graham cracker crumbs	1 cup	250 mL
Brown sugar, packed	½ cup	125 mL
Baking powder	2 tsp.	10 mL
Salt	½ tsp.	2 mL
Chopped cranberries	1 cup	250 mL
Raisins	1 cup	250 mL
Chopped walnuts	½ cup	125 mL
Grated orange rind	1 tbsp.	15 mL
Beaten egg	1	1
Orange juice	1 cup	250 mL
Cooking oil	⅓ cup	75 mL

Mix first five ingredients together in bowl.

Stir in cranberries, raisins, nuts and orange rind.

Add beaten egg, orange juice and oil. Stir until blended. Scrape into greased 9 × 5 × 3 inch (23 × 12 × 7 cm) loaf pan. Bake in 350°F (180°C) oven for 1 hour until inserted toothpick comes out clean. Let stand 10 minutes. Remove from pan to cool. Wrap when cool. Yield: 1 loaf.

CHERRY DATE LOAF

Makes a large, good loaf.

Butter or margarine	¼ cup	50 mL
Cut up dates	½ cup	125 mL
Baking soda	1 tsp.	5 mL
Boiling water	1 cup	250 mL
Vanilla	1 tsp.	5 mL
All purpose flour	2 cups	500 mL
Granulated sugar	1 cup	250 mL
Baking powder	1 tsp.	5 mL
Salt	½ tsp.	2 mL
Glazed cherries, halved	1 cup	250 mL
Chopped nuts	½ cup	125 mL
Beaten eggs	2	2

In medium bowl combine butter, dates and baking soda. Measure boiling water and pour over top. Add vanilla.

In second bowl combine flour, sugar, baking powder and salt. Stir. Add cherries and nuts. Stir in.

In mixing bowl beat eggs until frothy and light. Add date mixture. Stir to mix. Add flour-cherry mixture. Stir only until moistened. Spoon into greased 9 × 5 × 3 inch (23 × 12 × 7 cm) loaf pan. Bake in 350°F (180°C) oven for 1 hour. Test with toothpick. Cool 10 minutes. Remove from pan to finish cooling on rack. Store in plastic bag. Yield: 1 loaf.

Pare Pointer

If it weren't for that great blessing — money — many people wouldn't get a chance to communicate with their kids at all.

CRANBERRY ORANGE LOAF

An excellent flavor choice.

Butter or margarine	¼ cup	50 mL
Granulated sugar	1 cup	250 mL
Egg	1	1
Juice of 1 orange and water to make	¾ cup	175 mL
All purpose flour	2 cups	500 mL
Baking powder	1½ tsp.	10 mL
Baking soda	½ tsp.	2 mL
Salt	½ tsp.	2 mL
Grated rind of orange	1	1
Whole cranberries, fresh or frozen	1½ cups	375 mL
Chopped pecans or walnuts	½ cup	125 mL

Put butter, sugar and egg in mixing bowl. Beat smooth. Stir in juice.

In second bowl measure in flour, baking powder, soda and salt. Stir in orange rind, cranberries and nuts. Empty all into batter stirring until moistened. Scrape into greased loaf pan 9 × 5 × 3 inch (23 × 12 × 7 cm). Bake in 350°F (180°C) oven for 1 hour. Test with toothpick trying not to poke a whole cranberry. Let stand 10 minutes. Remove from pan. Cool on cake rack. Wrap. It tastes even better the next day. Yield: 1 loaf.

Variation: Add ½ cup (50 mL) chopped green cherries. Chop cranberries or leave whole.

Pictured on cover.

We all know snakes hiss, not snap. Except for the garter snake that is.

CRANBERRY BANANA LOAF

A subtle combination of flavors with a spicy tinge.

Butter or margarine, melted	¼ cup	50 mL
Granulated sugar	1 cup	250 mL
Eggs	2	2
Mashed very ripe bananas (2 or 3)	¾ cup	175 mL
Chopped cranberries, fresh or frozen	1 cup	250 mL
All purpose flour	1½ cups	375 mL
Baking powder	1½ tsp.	10 mL
Baking soda	½ tsp.	2 mL
Salt	½ tsp.	2 mL
Cinnamon	½ tsp.	2 mL

Put butter, sugar and 1 egg in mixing bowl. Beat until smooth. Beat in second egg. Stir in banana and cranberries.

Using another bowl put flour, baking powder, soda, salt and cinnamon. Stir together well. Add all at once to banana mixture. Stir only to moisten. Scrape into greased 9 × 5 × 3 inch (23 × 12 × 7 cm) loaf pan. Bake in 350°F (180°C) oven for 1 hour until it tests done. Let stand 10 minutes. Remove from pan to cake rack to cool. Wrap. Yield: 1 loaf.

Pictured on page 35.

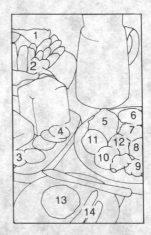

DATE PINEAPPLE LOAF

A delightful combination, lighter colored than most date loaves.

Crushed pineapple with juice	1 cup	250 mL
Chopped dates	1 cup	250 mL
Baking soda	1 tsp.	5 mL
Butter or margarine	¼ cup	50 mL
Honey (or sugar ¾ cup, 175 mL)	½ cup	125 mL
Egg	1	1
Vanilla	1 tsp.	5 mL
All purpose flour	2 cups	500 mL
Baking powder	2 tsp.	10 mL
Salt	½ tsp.	2 mL

Heat pineapple in saucepan until hot. Remove from heat. Add dates and soda. Stir. Cool.

In mixing bowl beat butter, honey, egg and vanilla. Stir in date mixture.

In smaller bowl mix flour, baking powder and salt. Stir to mix then pour into batter. Stir to moisten. Spoon into greased loaf pan 9 × 5 × 3 inch (23 × 12 × 7 cm). Bake in 350°F (180°C) oven for 1 hour or until it tests done. Let stand 10 minutes. Remove loaf. Cool and wrap. Yield: 1 loaf.

Paré Pointer

When everything is coming your way, better check what lane you're in.

DATE LOAF

Extra moist, extra yummy.

Dates, cut up	1¼ cups	300 mL
Boiling water	¾ cup	175 mL
Baking soda	1 tsp.	5 mL
Egg	1	1
Packed brown sugar	¾ cup	175 mL
Salt	¾ tsp.	3 mL
Vanilla	1 tsp.	5 mL
All purpose flour	1½ cups	375 mL
Baking powder	1 tsp.	5 mL
Chopped walnuts	½ cup	125 mL
Melted butter or margarine	¼ cup	50 mL

In small bowl put cut up dates, boiling water and soda. Stir and cool.

Beat egg lightly. Add sugar, salt and vanilla. Beat to mix. Stir in date mixture.

Mix flour and baking powder together then pour into date mixture. Stir to mix. Stir in nuts and melted butter. Pour into greased 9 × 5 × 3 inch (23 × 12 × 7 cm) loaf pan. Let stand for 20 minutes, then bake in 350°F (180°C) oven for 1 hour. Let stand for 10 minutes. Remove from pan. Cool and wrap. Yield: 1 loaf.

DATE GRAHAM LOAF

This is a dark, good loaf.

Chopped dates	1 cup	250 mL
Boiling water	1 cup	250 mL
Baking soda	1 tsp.	5 mL
Egg, beaten	1	1
Melted butter or margarine	2 tbsp.	30 mL
Granulated sugar	¾ cup	175 mL
Vanilla	1 tsp.	5 mL
All purpose flour	1 cup	250 mL
Graham flour	1 cup	250 mL
Baking powder	2 tsp.	10 mL
Salt	½ tsp.	2 mL
Chopped walnuts	½ cup	125 mL

(continued on next page)

In large bowl combine dates, water and soda. Let cool a little.

Beat egg, butter, sugar and vanilla. Stir into date mixture.

Combine remaining 5 ingredients. Mix together well. Stir into date batter. Scrape into greased 9 × 5 × 3 inch (23 × 12 × 7 cm) loaf pan. Bake for 1 hour in 350°F (180°C) oven. Test with toothpick. Remove from oven to stand 10 minutes before transferring from pan to rack. Cool and wrap. Yield: 1 loaf.

Pictured on page 35.

FAVORITE NUT

It will be your favorite nut too. Superb flavor.

Packaged cream cheese	8 oz.	250 g
Granulated sugar	⅓ cup	75 mL
Egg	1	1
Eggs	2	2
Cooking oil	½ cup	125 mL
Milk	½ cup	125 mL
Grated lemon rind	1 tsp.	5 mL
All purpose flour	2¼ cups	550 mL
Granulated sugar	⅓ cup	75 mL
Packed brown sugar	⅓ cup	75 mL
Baking soda	1 tsp.	5 mL
Salt	1 tsp.	5 mL
Chopped walnuts	1 cup	250 mL

Have cream cheese at room temperature. Beat cheese, sugar and one egg together well. Set aside.

Beat remaining two eggs in mixing bowl until frothy. Mix in oil, milk and lemon rind.

In another bowl measure in remaining six ingredients. Stir to mix well. Pour all at once into egg-milk mixture. Stir until moistened. Spoon ½ batter into greased loaf pan 9 × 5 × 3 inch (23 × 12 × 7 cm). Spoon on cheese mixture. Cover with remaining batter by dropping small spoonfuls here and there. Bake in 350°F (180°C) oven for 1 hour until it tests done. Cool 15 minutes in pan before turning out very carefully to rack. Yield: 1 loaf.

Pictured on page 35.

DATE MOCHA LOAF

A different loaf and delicious.

Chopped dates	1½ cups	375 mL
Hot coffee	1 cup	250 mL
Baking soda	1 tsp.	5 mL
Butter or margarine, melted	¼ cup	50 mL
Egg	1	1
Granulated sugar	1 cup	250 mL
All purpose flour	2 cups	500 mL
Baking powder	2 tsp.	10 mL
Salt	½ tsp.	2 mL
Chopped nuts	½ cup	125 mL

Combine dates, coffee and soda in bowl. Cool.

Beat melted butter, egg and sugar in large second bowl. Stir in date mixture.

In third bowl stir flour, baking powder, salt and nuts together. Pour all over batter. Stir to moisten. Spoon into greased loaf pan 9 × 5 × 3 inch (23 × 12 × 7 cm). Bake in 350°F (180°C) oven for 1 hour or until it tests done. Let stand 10 minutes. Remove from pan. Cool and wrap. Yield: 1 loaf.

FRUIT BREAD

A very pretty loaf with fruit in a light colored background.

All purpose flour	2 cups	500 mL
Granulated sugar	¾ cup	175 mL
Baking powder	3½ tsp.	20 mL
Salt	¾ tsp.	5 mL
Diced candied pineapple	¼ cup	50 mL
Raisins or currants	½ cup	125 mL
Chopped glazed cherries	½ cup	125 mL
Eggs	2	2
Milk	1 cup	250 mL
Cooking oil	¼ cup	50 mL

(continued on next page)

In large bowl measure in first seven ingredients. Stir thoroughly. Make a well in center.

Put eggs in small bowl. Beat until frothy. Mix in milk and oil. Pour into well. Stir just to moisten. Pour into greased loaf pan 9 × 5 × 3 inch (23 × 12 × 7 cm). Bake in 350°F (180°C) oven for 1 hour. Let cool in pan 10 minutes then remove. Yield: 1 loaf.

Pictured on page 35.

HARVEST LOAF

A brown loaf with dark brown dots. Very tasty.

Butter or margarine	½ cup	125 mL
Granulated sugar	1 cup	250 mL
Eggs	2	2
Canned pumpkin	1 cup	250 mL
All purpose flour	2 cups	500 mL
Baking powder	1½ tsp.	10 mL
Baking soda	½ tsp.	2 mL
Salt	½ tsp.	2 mL
Cinnamon	½ tsp.	3 mL
Nutmeg	½ tsp.	2 mL
Ginger	½ tsp.	2 mL
Semi-sweet chocolate chips	1 cup	250 mL
Chopped nuts	½ cup	125 mL

Cream butter and sugar in mixing bowl. Beat in eggs one at a time until smooth. Stir in pumpkin.

In another bowl combine remaining nine ingredients. Stir to mix then pour into mixing bowl. Stir all together until just moistened. Spoon into greased 9 × 5 × 3 inch (23 × 12 × 7 cm) loaf pan. Bake in 350°F (180°C) oven for 1 hour until it tests done. After 10 minutes cooling time, turn loaf out to cool on a rack. Wrap. Yield: 1 loaf.

FRUIT AND NUT LOAF

A fruited light colored loaf. Very pretty when cut.

Butter or margarine	½ cup	125 mL
Granulated sugar	1 cup	250 mL
Eggs	2	2
Milk	1 cup	250 mL
Vanilla flavoring	1 tsp.	5 mL
Almond flavoring	½ tsp.	3 mL
All purpose flour	2⅛ cups	525 mL
Baking powder	2 tsp.	10 mL
Salt	½ tsp.	2 mL
Glazed fruit	¾ cup	175 mL
Raisins or currants	¾ cup	175 mL
Chopped almonds	½ cup	125 mL

Cream butter and sugar together. Beat in eggs one at a time. Beat smooth. Stir in milk, vanilla and almond flavoring.

In large bowl combine flour, baking powder and salt. Stir in fruit, raisins and nuts. Add all at once to first bowl. Stir only to moisten. Turn into greased loaf pan 9×5×3 inch (23×12×7 cm). Bake for 1 hour in 350°F (180°C) oven until it tests done. Let stand 10 minutes. Remove from pan. Cool. Wrap. Yield: 1 loaf.

LEMON LOAF

A favorite flavor of most people. The glaze makes the loaf.

Butter or margarine	½ cup	125 mL
Granulated sugar	1 cup	250 mL
Eggs	2	2
Milk	½ cup	125 mL
All purpose flour	1½ cups	375 mL
Baking powder	1 tsp.	5 mL
Salt	½ tsp.	2 mL
Grated rind of lemon	1	1

(continued on next page)

In large bowl, cream butter, sugar and 1 egg. Beat in second egg. Blend in milk.

In second bowl thoroughly stir flour, baking powder, salt and lemon rind. Pour over batter. Stir to moisten. Spoon into greased loaf pan 9 × 5 × 3 inch (23 × 12 × 7 cm). Bake in 350°F (180°C) oven for 1 hour until it tests done. Remove from oven and glaze. Cool in pan 10 minutes. Remove from pan. Cool and wrap. Yield: 1 loaf.

GLAZE:

Juice of lemon	1	1
Granulated sugar	¼ cup	50 mL

Combine lemon juice and sugar in small saucepan. Heat and stir to dissolve sugar. Spoon evenly over top of hot loaf.

LUXURY LOAF

Try this for a smooth textured, different loaf.

Butter or margarine	1 cup	225 mL
Granulated sugar	1 cup	225 mL
Eggs	5	5
Vanilla	1 tsp.	5 mL
Grated rind of orange	1	1
Orange juice	¼ cup	50 mL
All purpose flour	2 cups	450 mL
Baking powder	1 tsp.	5 mL
Salt	½ tsp.	2 mL
Nutmeg	¼ tsp.	2 mL
Grated semi-sweet chocolate	4 oz.	113 g
Chopped nuts	⅓ cup	75 mL

Cream butter and sugar together well until fluffy. Beat in eggs one at a time, beating well after each addition. Stir in vanilla, rind and juice.

Put flour, baking powder, salt and nutmeg into another bowl. Stir in grated chocolate and nuts. Pour into first bowl. Stir all together until moistened. Spoon into greased loaf pan 9 × 5 × 3 inch (23 × 12 × 7 cm). Bake in 325°F (170°C) for 1 hour and 15 minutes until a toothpick inserted in center comes out clean. Let stand 10 minutes. Remove loaf from pan to cool on cake rack. Wrap. Yield: 1 loaf.

Pictured on cover.

MARMALADE LOAF

Although the fruit is optional it adds to both the looks and flavor.

Eggs	2	2
Granulated sugar	¾ cup	175 mL
Melted butter or margarine	¼ cup	50 mL
Milk	¾ cup	175 mL
Orange marmalade	½ cup	125 mL
Vinegar	2 tbsp.	30 mL
All purpose flour	2½ cups	625 mL
Baking powder	1 tsp.	5 mL
Baking soda	1 tsp.	5 mL
Salt	1 tsp.	5 mL
Grated grind of part of lemon	½	½
Grated rind of part of orange	½	½
Glazed mixed fruit (optional)	1 cup	250 mL

Beat eggs, sugar and butter together. Stir in milk, marmalade and vinegar.

Combine all the remaining ingredients in another bowl. Stir well to distribute fruit. Pour all at once into batter. Stir to moisten. Scrape into greased loaf pan 9 × 5 × 3 inch (23 × 12 × 7 cm). Bake in 350°F (180°C) oven for 1 hour until it tests done. Cool 10 minutes. Remove from pan to rack to cool. Wrap to store. Yield: 1 loaf.

Note: Sprinkle dark brown sugar over top before baking, about 2 tbsp. (30 mL).

It's a good idea to keep your words gentle and sweet — you might have to eat them one day.

Slices into a very pretty plateful. Makes a large loaf.

Eggs	3	3
Granulated sugar	1 cup	250 mL
Cooking oil	½ cup	125 mL
Milk	½ cup	125 mL
Vanilla	1 tsp.	5 mL
Grated carrot	1 cup	250 mL
All purpose flour	2½ cups	625 mL
Baking powder	1 tsp.	5 mL
Baking soda	1 tsp.	5 mL
Cinnamon	½ tsp.	3 mL
Salt	½ tsp.	2 mL
Coconut, flaked or medium	1 cup	250 mL
Glazed cherries, cut up	½ cup	125 mL
Raisins	½ cup	125 mL
Chopped walnuts or almonds	½ cup	125 mL

In a large bowl beat eggs until frothy. Add sugar and oil. Beat to blend. Stir in milk, vanilla and carrot.

In another bowl, combine all nine remaining ingredients. Mix well to combine evenly. Pour all at once over batter. Stir to moisten. Turn into greased loaf pan 9 × 5 × 3 inch (23 × 12 × 7 cm). Bake in 350°F (180°C) oven for 1 hour until it tests done. Cool 10 minutes. Remove from pan. Cool and wrap. Yield: 1 loaf.

Pictured on page 35.

MINCE BREAD

Great to use up leftover mincemeat.

Cooking oil	¼ cup	50 mL
Granulated sugar	½ cup	125 mL
Egg	1	1
Milk	½ cup	125 mL
Prepared mincemeat	1 cup	250 mL
All purpose flour	2 cups	500 mL
Baking powder	3 tsp.	15 mL
Salt	½ tsp.	2 mL
Cinnamon	½ tsp.	2 mL
Chopped walnuts	½ cup	125 mL

Beat together oil, sugar, egg and milk. Stir in mincemeat.

In another bowl combine remaining five ingredients. Stir together well. Pour all at once into batter. Stir only to moisten. Scrape into greased loaf pan 9 × 5 × 3 inch (23 × 12 × 7 cm). Bake in center of 350°F (180°C) oven for 60-70 minutes until it tests done. Let stand 10 minutes. Turn out of pan to cake rack. Cool and wrap. Yield: 1 loaf.

MINCE PUMPKIN LOAF

This large loaf combines the two flavors superbly.

Melted butter or margarine	½ cup	125 mL
Granulated sugar	¾ cup	175 mL
Eggs	2	2
Canned pumpkin	1 cup	250 mL
Prepared mincement	1 cup	250 mL
All purpose flour	2 cups	500 mL
Baking powder	1 tsp.	5 mL
Baking soda	1 tsp.	5 mL
Cinnamon	½ tsp.	3 mL
Nutmeg	½ tsp.	2 mL
Ginger	½ tsp.	2 mL
Salt	½ tsp.	2 mL

(continued on next page)

In large bowl combine butter, sugar and eggs. Beat until smooth. Stir in pumpkin and mincemeat.

In different bowl combine all remaining ingredients. Stir to mix well. Pour over batter. Stir until moistened. Pour into greased 9 × 5 × 3 inch (23 × 12 × 7 cm) loaf pan. Bake in 350°F (180°C) oven for 1 hour or until it tests done. Let stand 10 minutes. Remove from pan. Cool and wrap. Yield: 1 loaf.

Pictured on cover.

PEANUT BUTTER LOAF

Rich colored loaf with flavor to match.

Butter or margarine	¼ cup	50 mL
Peanut butter	¾ cup	175 mL
Granulated sugar	1 cup	250 mL
Eggs	2	2
Milk	1 cup	250 mL
Vanilla	1 tsp.	5 mL
All purpose flour	2 cups	500 mL
Baking powder	1 tsp.	5 mL
Baking soda	½ tsp.	2 mL
Salt	½ tsp.	2 mL
Chopped dates	1½ cups	375 mL

Cream butter, peanut butter and sugar together. Beat in eggs one at a time beating until smooth. Stir in milk and vanilla.

In second bowl combine and stir remaining five ingredients. Add to first bowl, stirring until just mixed. Pour into greased loaf pan 9 × 5 × 3 inch (23 × 12 × 7 cm). Bake in 350°F (180°C) oven for 1 hour or until it tests done. Let loaf stand for 10 minutes. Transfer from pan to rack. Cool and wrap. Serve with Creamed Orange Spread. Yield: 1 loaf.

ORANGE LOAF

The easiest of the orange loaves to make.

Butter or margarine	½ cup	125 mL
Granulated sugar	1 cup	250 mL
Eggs	2	2
Grated rind from orange	1	1
Juice from orange plus water if needed	½ cup	125 mL
All purpose flour	2 cups	500 mL
Baking powder	2 tsp.	10 mL
Salt	½ tsp.	2 mL
Chopped walnuts (optional)	½ cup	125 mL

Put butter, sugar and 1 egg into mixing bowl. Beat together. Beat in second egg. Stir in rind and juice.

In another bowl put flour, baking powder, salt and nuts. Stir well and pour into mixing bowl. Stir until moistened. Turn into greased $9 \times 5 \times 3$ inch ($23 \times 12 \times 7$ cm) loaf pan. Bake in 350°F (180°C) oven for 1 hour. Test with toothpick. Pour glaze over top. Let stand 10 minutes before removing loaf to rack to cool. Wrap to store. Yield: 1 loaf.

GLAZE:

Juice from orange	1	1
Granulated sugar	¼ cup	50 mL

Combine orange juice with sugar in small saucepan. Heat and stir to dissolve sugar. Spoon over hot loaf.

Pictured on page 35.

Good, spicy and nice looking.

Egg	1	1
Cooking oil	½ cup	125 mL
Granulated sugar	1 cup	250 mL
Grated zucchini	1 cup	250 mL
Vanilla	½ tsp.	2 mL
All purpose flour	1½ cups	375 mL
Baking powder	½ tsp.	3 mL
Baking soda	1 tsp.	5 mL
Salt	½ tsp.	2 mL
Cinnamon	¾ tsp.	3 mL
Nutmeg	½ tsp.	2 mL
Coconut	½ cup	125 mL
Chopped walnuts	½ cup	125 mL
Currants or raisins, that have been boiled in 1 cup (250 mL) water for 2 minutes and drained	½ cup	125 mL

In mixing bowl beal egg, oil and sugar. Stir in zucchini and vanilla.

In another bowl, measure all nine remaining ingredients. Stir to combine thoroughly. Pour all at once over batter in mixing bowl. Stir to moisten. Turn into greased 9 × 5 × 3 inch (23 × 12 × 7 cm) loaf pan. Bake in 350°F (180°C) oven for 1 hour until an inserted toothpick comes out clean. Cool in pan 10 minutes. Turn out on rack. Cool and wrap. Cuts better tomorrow. Yield: 1 loaf.

Pare Pointer

Should there be turtle in turtle soup? After all there is no horse in horseradish.

ORANGE PUMPKIN LOAF

Try with an orange cream spread, butter or leave plain. It is a moist loaf.

Butter or margarine	⅓ cup	75 mL
Granulated sugar	1⅓ cups	325 mL
Eggs	2	2
Canned pumpkin	1 cup	250 mL
Water	⅓ cup	75 mL
Medium size orange, ground	1	1
All purpose flour	2 cups	500 mL
Baking soda	1 tsp.	5 mL
Baking powder	½ tsp.	2 mL
Salt	¾ tsp	3 mL
Cinnamon	½ tsp.	2 mL
Cloves	½ tsp.	2 mL
Chopped nuts	½ cup	125 mL
Raisins or chopped dates	½ cup	125 mL

Cream butter and sugar together well. Add eggs. Beat lightly. Add pumpkin and water. Stir.

Cut and remove seeds from orange. Put in blender or grinder and grind complete orange including peel. Stir into batter.

Combine next eight ingredients in bowl mixing well. Stir into batter. Spoon into greased loaf pan 9 × 5 × 3 inch (23 × 12 × 7 cm). Bake in 350°F (180°C) oven for 1 hour. Test with toothpick. Let stand 10 minutes. Remove from pan. Cool and wrap. Yield: 1 loaf.

Make it with or without cherries, with or without the glaze, it is good either way.

Poppy seeds	¼ cup	50 mL
Milk	¾ cup	175 mL
Butter or margarine	½ cup	125 mL
Granulated sugar	¾ cup	175 mL
Eggs	2	2
Lemon juice	1 tsp.	5 mL
All purpose flour	2 cups	500 mL
Baking powder	2½ tsp.	15 mL
Salt	½ tsp.	3 mL
Maraschino cherries, well drained and halved	½ cup	125 mL

Put poppy seeds and milk in small bowl. Let stand for 30 minutes.

Combine butter, sugar and 1 egg in mixing bowl. Beat well. Add second egg and lemon juice. Beat until smooth. Stir in poppy seed mixture.

Measure flour, baking powder, salt and cherries together in small bowl. Mix well. Stir into batter until just moistened. Pour into greased 9 × 5 × 3 inch (23 × 12 × 7 cm) loaf pan. Bake in 350°F (180°C) oven for 1 hour. Pour glaze over top. Cool 10 minutes before removing from pan to cool on cake rack. Wrap. Yield: 1 loaf.

BROWN SUGAR GLAZE

Brown sugar	5 tbsp.	75 mL
Butter or margarine	2 tbsp.	30 mL
Cream or milk	2 tbsp.	30 mL
Crushed nuts	1-2 tbsp.	15-30 mL

Combine sugar, butter and cream in small saucepan. Bring to boil and simmer 3 minutes. Spoon over hot loaf. Sprinkle with nuts.

Pictured on page 35.

LEMON RAISIN LOAF

A large, moist loaf and really good! A must to try.

Boiling water	1 cup	250 mL
Raisins	1½ cups	375
Baking soda	1 tsp.	5 mL
Butter or margarine, softened	½ cup	125 mL
Brown sugar, packed	1½ cups	300 mL
Egg	1	1
Grated rind of lemon	1	1
Juice of lemon	1	1
All–purpose flour	2½ cups	625 mL
Baking powder	1 tsp.	5 mL
Salt	½ tsp.	2 mL
Chopped nuts	½ cup	125 mL

Pour water over raisins and baking soda in saucepan. Bring to boil. Remove from heat. Cool.

Beat butter, sugar and egg together well. Stir in lemon rind, juice and cooled raisin mixture.

In another bowl stir together flour, baking powder, salt and chopped nuts. Add all at once into batter, stirring until combined. Pour into greased loaf pan 9 x 5 x 3 inch (23 x 12 x 7 cm). Bake for about 1 hour in 350°F (180°C) oven. Test with toothpick. Let stand for 10 minutes before removing from pan to cool on rack. Wrap. It cuts better the next day. Yield: 1 loaf.

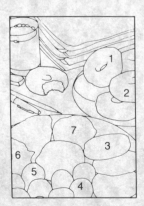

PUMPKIN TEA BREAD

A large loaf which has orange in it.

Butter or margarine	½ cup	125 mL
Granulated sugar	1½ cups	375 mL
Eggs	2	2
Canned pumpkin	1 cup	250 mL
Grated rind of orange	1 tbsp.	15 mL
Orange juice	¼ cup	50 mL
All purpose flour	2¼ cups	550 mL
Baking powder	½ tsp.	3 mL
Baking soda	2 tsp.	10 mL
Salt	½ tsp.	3 mL
Cinnamon	½ tsp.	3 mL
Cloves	½ tsp.	2 mL
Chopped nuts	½ cup	125 mL
Chopped dates	½ cup	125 mL

In mixing bowl cream butter, sugar and 1 egg. Beat in second egg until smooth. Mix in pumpkin, rind and juice.

In another bowl measure and stir well all remaining ingredients. Pour all at once into batter in mixing bowl. Stir only to moisten. Pour into greased loaf pan 9 × 5 × 3 inch (23 × 12 × 7 cm). Bake in 350°F (180°C) oven for about 1 hour or until an inserted toothpick comes out clean. Cool in pan 10 minutes. Remove loaf from pan to rack. Cool and wrap. Yield: 1 loaf.

Be careful buying clothes when you are down in the dumps. Try a better location.

PINEAPPLE BREAD

A moist, tasty loaf. Try a cream cheese spread.

Eggs	2	2
Melted butter or margarine	½ cup	125 mL
Granulated sugar	1 cup	250 mL
Crushed pineapple with juice	1 cup	250 mL
Vanilla	1 tsp.	5 mL
All purpose flour	2½ cups	625 mL
Baking powder	3 tsp.	15 mL
Baking soda	½ tsp.	3 mL
Salt	¾ tsp.	3 mL
Chopped walnuts or pecans	½ cup	125 mL

Beat eggs slightly. Add butter and sugar. Beat smooth. Stir in pineapple and vanilla.

In separate bowl put flour, baking powder, soda, salt and nuts. Stir well and pour into pineapple mixture. Stir to moisten. Pour into greased loaf pan 9 × 5 × 3 inch (23 × 12 × 7 cm). Bake in 350°F (180°C) oven for 1 hour. Test with toothpick. Let stand 10 minutes. Remove from pan. Cool and wrap. Yield: 1 loaf.

PINEAPPLE CHEESE LOAF: Omit nuts. Add 1 cup (250 mL) grated sharp cheddar cheese.

PINEAPPLE RAISIN/DATE LOAF: Add 1 cup (250 mL) raisins or chopped dates.

Better to have loved a short person than never to have loved a tall.

This good loaf is large and tender.

Eggs	2	2
Cooking oil	½ cup	125 mL
Granulated sugar	1 cup	250 mL
Shredded zucchini, unpeeled	1 cup	250 mL
Crushed pineapple, drained	½ cup	125 mL
Vanilla	1 tsp.	5 mL
All purpose flour	2 cups	500 mL
Baking soda	1 tsp.	5 mL
Baking powder	½ tsp.	3 mL
Salt	½ tsp.	2 mL
Cinnamon	¾ tsp.	3 mL
Nutmeg	¼ tsp.	2 mL
Chopped nuts	½ cup	125 mL

Beat eggs, oil and sugar. Stir in zucchini, pineapple and vanilla.

Measure remaining seven ingredients in another bowl. Stir to distribute. Pour all at once into batter. Stir to moisten. Pour into greased loaf pan 9 × 5 × 3 inch (23 × 12 × 7 cm). Bake in 350°F (180°C) oven for 1 hour until it tests done. Cool for 10 minutes. Turn loaf out of pan to cool on rack. Wrap. Cut in thin slices and spread with butter. Yield: 1 loaf.

Note: Adding 1 cup (250 mL) raisins to above is a nice variation.

One good thing about smog is at least you can see what you're breathing.

DATE ORANGE BREAD

The orange flavor perks up the date flavor.

Egg, beaten	1	1
Butter or margarine, softened	2 tbsp.	30 mL
Granulated sugar	1 cup	250 mL
Grated rind of oranges	2	2
Juice of 2 oranges and boiling water to make	1 cup	250 mL
Vanilla	1 tsp.	5 mL
All purpose flour	2 cups	500 mL
Baking powder	1 tsp.	5 mL
Baking soda	1 tsp.	5 mL
Salt	¾ tsp.	3 mL
Chopped walnuts or brazils	½ cup	125 mL
Chopped dates	1 cup	250 mL

Beat egg slightly. Add butter and sugar. Beat smooth. Add rind and juice. Stir in vanilla.

Using another bowl put flour, baking powder, soda and salt. Stir in nuts and dates. Pour over batter. Stir to moisten. Spoon into greased loaf pan 9 × 5 × 3 inch (23 × 12 × 7 cm). Bake in 350°F (180°C) oven for 1 hour until it tests done. Cool 10 minutes. Remove from pan. Finish cooling and wrap. Yield: 1 loaf.

ZUCCHINI LOAF

A large, tender loaf.

Eggs	2	2
Cooking oil	½ cup	125 mL
Granulated sugar	1 cup	250 mL
Grated zucchini, unpeeled	1 cup	250 mL
Vanilla	1 tsp.	5 mL
All purpose flour	2 cups	500 mL
Baking powder	1 tsp.	5 mL
Baking soda	1 tsp.	5 mL
Salt	½ tsp.	2 mL
Cinnamon	1 tsp.	5 mL

(continued on next page)

Beat eggs until frothy. Beat in oil and sugar. Add zucchini. Stir in vanilla.

In separate bowl put remaining five dry ingredients. Stir well and pour into zucchini mixture. Stir to moisten. Pour into greased loaf pan 9 × 5 × 3 inch (23 × 12 × 7 cm). Bake for 50-60 minutes in 350°F (180°C) oven until a toothpick inserted in the center comes out clean. Let stand 10 minutes. Remove from pan. Cool on rack. Wrap. Yield: 1 loaf.

THE GREAT PUMPKIN

The cream cheese contributes to the excellence of this loaf.

Cream cheese, package	4 oz.	125 g
Butter or margarine	¼ cup	50 mL
Granulated sugar	1¼ cups	300 mL
Eggs	2	2
Canned pumpkin	1 cup	250 mL
All purpose flour	1¾ cups	425 mL
Baking soda	1 tsp.	5 mL
Baking powder	¼ tsp.	1 mL
Salt	½ tsp.	2 mL
Cinnamon	½ tsp.	2 mL
Cloves	¼ tsp.	1 mL
Chopped walnuts	½ cup	125 mL

Put softened cheese, butter and sugar in mixing bowl. Cream together well. Beat in eggs one at a time until blended. Mix in pumpkin.

In another bowl combine all seven remaining ingredients. Stir until thoroughly mixed. Pour all at once over batter. Stir just enough to moisten. Turn into greased 9 × 5 × 3 inch (23 × 12 × 7 cm) loaf pan. Bake in 350°F (180°C) oven for 60-70 minutes until inserted toothpick comes out clean. Cool 10 minutes in pan. Remove to rack to finish cooling. Yield: 1 loaf.

RAISIN LOAF

This light colored small loaf comes from New Zealand.

Butter or margarine	¼ cup	50 mL
Granulated sugar	¾ cup	175 mL
Eggs	2	2
Milk	1 cup	250 mL
Vanilla	1 tsp.	5 mL
All purpose flour	2 cups	500 mL
Baking powder	2 tsp.	10 mL
Salt	½ tsp.	2 mL
Raisins, light color	½ cup	125 mL
Raisins, dark color	½ cup	125 mL

Put butter, sugar and 1 egg in large bowl. Beat well. Beat in second egg. Stir in milk and vanilla.

In another bowl measure in flour, baking powder and salt. Stir in raisins. Pour all at once into batter. Stir to moisten only. Spoon into greased loaf pan 9 × 5 × 3 inch (23 × 12 × 7 cm). Bake in 350°F (180°C) oven for 1 hour or until it tests done. Cool 10 minutes. Turn out of pan. Cool on rack. Wrap to store. Allow to ripen a day or two to improve flavor. Serve buttered. Yield: 1 loaf.

STRAWBERRY BANANA LOAF

A winning combination.

Eggs	2	2
Cooking oil	¼ cup	50 mL
Granulated sugar	1 cup	250 mL
Mashed strawberries	½ cup	125 mL
Mashed banana	½ cup	125 mL
All purpose flour	1¾ cup	425 mL
Rolled oats	½ cup	125 mL
Baking powder	2 tsp.	10 mL
Baking soda	½ tsp.	3 mL
Salt	½ tsp.	2 mL

(continued on next page)

In mixing bowl beat eggs until frothy. Stir in oil, sugar, strawberries and bananas.

In separate bowl combine flour, oats, baking powder, soda and salt. Stir to distribute evenly, then add all of it to first bowl. Stir to moisten. Turn into greased 9 × 5 × 3 inch (23 × 12 × 7 cm) loaf pan. Bake in 350°F (180°C) oven for about 1 hour until toothpick inserted in center comes out clean. Cool for 10 minutes then remove from pan to cool on rack. Wrap well and allow to ripen one day. Yield: 1 loaf.

TOFFEE LOAF

Sweetened condensed milk gives this favorite loaf its distinctive toffee flavor.

Sweetened condensed milk	11 oz.	300 mL
Water	1 cup	225 mL
Butter or margarine	1 cup	250 mL
Raisins	1¼ cup	275 mL
Currants	½ cup	125 mL
Chopped nuts	1 cup	250 mL
All-purpose flour	2 cups	450 mL
Baking soda	1 tsp.	5 mL
Salt	⅛ tsp.	0.5 mL

Put condensed milk and water into large saucepan. Stir. Heat over medium heat until it boils. Simmer for 3 minutes. Stir frequently to prevent sticking. Remove from heat.

Stir in raisins, currants and dates. Let stand until warm.

Mix flour, baking soda and salt together and add. Stir to mix. Turn into greased 9 × 5 inch (22 × 10 cm) loaf pan. Bake in 325° F (160° C) oven for about 2 hours. Cover with foil half way through baking if top is getting dark. Let cool in pan 5 minutes. Remove to cool on rack.

BISHOP'S BREAD

Rich looking. Rich tasting.

Egg	1	1
Granulated sugar	½ cup	125 mL
Cooking oil	¼ cup	50 mL
Vanilla	1 tsp.	5 mL
Sour milk (1 tbsp., 15 mL, vinegar plus milk)	1 cup	250 mL
All purpose flour	2 cups	500 mL
Baking soda	½ tsp.	3 mL
Salt	½ tsp.	3 mL
Chopped walnuts	½ cup	125 mL
Chopped glazed cherries	½ cup	125 mL
Raisins or currants	½ cup	125 mL
Semi-sweet chocolate chips	½ cup	125 mL

Beat egg in mixing bowl until frothy. Add sugar, oil and vanilla. Beat to blend. Mix in sour milk.

In another bowl measure in flour, soda and salt. Stir to mix well. Add walnuts, cherries, raisins and chips. Mix together. Add all at once to liquid batter. Stir only to combine. Turn into greased loaf pan 9 × 5 × 3 inch (23 × 12 × 7 cm). Bake in 350°F (180°C) for 1 hour or until it tests done. Let stand 10 minutes. Remove from pan to cool on rack. Wrap to store. Cut "tomorrow". Yield 1 loaf.

Pictured on cover.

Five hundred hares got out of the rabbit farm. Police had to comb the area.

Both orange and prune flavor can be tasted.

Cooking oil	3 tbsp.	50 mL
Granulated sugar	⅔ cup	150 mL
Egg	1	1
Vanilla	½ tsp.	2 mL
Medium orange, ground	⅔ cup	150 mL
Orange juice	½ cup	125 mL
Stewed pitted prunes, chopped	1 cup	250 mL
All purpose flour	2 cups	500 mL
Baking powder	2½ tsp.	15 mL
Baking soda	½ tsp.	3 mL
Salt	½ tsp.	3 mL
Chopped walnuts	½ cup	125 mL

Beat oil, sugar and egg in large bowl until smooth. Stir in vanilla. Grind orange including rind (or use blender). Measure ⅔ cup. Add and stir. Mix in juice and prunes.

In second bowl measure flour, baking powder, soda, salt and nuts. Stir well. Empty into first bowl of batter. Stir to moisten. Turn into greased loaf pan 9 × 5 × 3 inch (23 × 12 × 7 cm). Bake in 350°F (180°C) oven for 1 hour until it tests done. Cool 10 minutes. Transfer from pan to cool on rack. Wrap. Yield: 1 loaf.

Pictured on cover.

Just because the teacher is going to teach Junior how to draw is no reason to let him take his toy guns to school.

ANGEL BISCUITS

Delicious and yeasty with no waiting for them to rise.

Granulated yeast	¼ oz.	8 g
Warm water	¼ cup	50 mL
All purpose flour	5 cups	1.25 L
Granulated sugar	3 tbsp.	50 mL
Baking powder	3 tsp.	15 mL
Baking soda	1 tsp.	5 mL
Salt	1 tsp.	5 mL
Butter or margarine	1 cup	250 mL
Buttermilk	2 cups	500 mL

Combine yeast in warm water. Set aside to dissolve 10 minutes.

Measure flour, sugar, baking powder, soda, salt and butter into large bowl. Cut in shortening until crumbly. Stir in yeast and buttermilk. Knead just enough to make dough hold together. Roll on floured surface ¾ inch (2 cm) thick. Cut with biscuit cutter. Bake on ungreased cookie sheet in 400°F (200°C) oven for 15 minutes. Yield: 2½ dozen biscuits.

BANANA BISCUITS

This delicate flavor goes well with a fruit salad.

All purpose flour	2 cups	500 mL
Granulated sugar	1 tbsp.	15 mL
Baking powder	2 tsp.	10 mL
Baking soda	½ tsp.	2 mL
Salt	¾ tsp.	3 mL
Cold butter or margarine	¼ cup	50 mL
Cold milk	¾ cup	175 mL
Mashed banana (1 large)	½ cup	125 mL

(continued on next page)

In large bowl put flour, sugar, baking powder, soda and salt. Cut in butter until crumbly. Make a well in center.

Pour milk and banana into well. Stir to moisten. Drop by spoonfuls onto greased cookie sheet. Bake in 400°F (200°C) oven for 15-20 minutes. Serve hot with butter and orange marmalade or peanut butter. Makes 15 biscuits.

Pictured on page 53.

BEST CHEESE BISCUITS

These taste as good as they look.

All purpose flour	2 cups	500 mL
Baking powder	4 tsp.	20 mL
Granulated sugar	2 tbsp.	30 mL
Salt	¾ tsp.	5 mL
Grated sharp Cheddar cheese	1 cup	250 mL
Cooking oil	⅓ cup	75 mL
Milk	¾ cup	175 mL

Measure first 4 dry ingredients together in bowl. Add grated cheese. Stir.

Add cooking oil and milk. Stir to form a soft ball of dough. Add more milk if needed to make dough soft. Turn out on lightly floured board and knead gently 8 to 10 times. Roll or pat ¾ to 1 inch (2 to 2.5 cm) thick. Cut with biscuit cutter. Place on ungreased cookie sheet close together for moist sides or one inch (2 cm) apart for crisp sides. Dab tops with milk for nicer browning. Bake in 425°F (220°C) oven for 15 minutes until nicely browned. Serve plain or with butter. Makes 1 dozen.

Note: Medium cheese can be used but it doesn't give as much flavor.

CRANBERRY BISCUITS: Omit cheese. Add 1 cup (250 mL) chopped cranberries, fresh or frozen. Pretty and tasty.

BRAN BISCUITS

Good with a salad meal or just coffee or tea.

All purpose flour	2 cups	500 mL
Granulated sugar	¼ cup	50 mL
Baking powder	4 tsp.	20 mL
Salt	½ tsp.	2 mL
Cold butter or margarine	½ cup	125 mL
Bran flakes	½ cup	125 mL
Chopped dates	½ cup	125 mL
Egg, beaten	1	1
Milk, cold	¾ cup	175 mL

In large bowl combine flour, sugar, baking powder and salt. Cut in butter until crumbly. Stir in bran flakes and dates. Make a well in the center.

Beat egg in small bowl until frothy. Mix in milk. Pour into well. Stir lightly to form a drop dough. If needed add more milk. Dough should be sticky. Drop by spoonful 1 inch (3 cm) apart on greased cookie sheet. Bake in 450°F (235°C) oven for 10-12 minutes. Serve hot with butter. Makes 16.

Pictured on page 53.

BUTTERSCOTCH BUNS

These are a picture in themselves. Just yummy! A snap to make.

Butter or margarine	⅓ cup	75 mL
Packed brown sugar	¾ cup	175 mL
Chopped nuts	⅓ cup	75 mL
All purpose flour	2 cups	500 mL
Granulated sugar	2 tbsp.	30 mL
Baking powder	4 tsp.	20 mL
Salt	1 tsp.	5 mL
Cold butter or margarine	¼ cup	50 mL
Milk	1 cup	250 mL

(continued on next page)

Cream butter and brown sugar together in small bowl. Nuts will be sprinkled later. Set aside.

In large bowl put flour, sugar, baking powder and salt. Cut in butter until crumbly. Make a well in center.

Pour milk into well. Stir to make a soft dough. Knead 8-10 times. Pat or roll out on lightly floured surface to 9 or 10 inch (23 to 25 cm) square. Spread with brown sugar mixture. Sprinkle with nuts. Roll up as for jelly roll. Pinch edge to seal. Cut into 12 slices. Place on greased 8 × 8 inch (20 × 20 cm) pan. Bake in 425°F (220°C) oven for 15-20 minutes. Invert over tray while hot. Yield: 12 butterscotch buns.

Pictured on page 53.

COTTAGE CHEESE BISCUITS

Serve with fruit, soup or salad.

All purpose flour	2 cups	500 mL
Baking powder	4 tsp.	20 mL
Salt	1 tsp.	5 mL
Parsley flakes (optional)	1 tbsp.	15 mL
Egg, beaten	1	1
Cottage cheese	1 cup	250 mL
Cooking oil	2 tbsp.	30 mL
Milk	¼ cup	50 mL

In mixing bowl put flour, baking powder, salt and parsley. Stir to combine. Make a well in center.

Beat egg in small bowl. Beat in cottage cheese. Add oil and milk. Stir and pour all at once into well. Stir to form soft dough. Turn out on lightly floured board. Knead gently 8-10 times. Pat or roll to ¾ inch (2 cm) thickness. Cut with floured cookie cutter. Arrange on ungreased baking sheet. Brushing tops with milk help them brown. Bake in 425°F (220°C) oven for 10-12 minutes. Yield: 1 dozen.

CRUNCHY DROP BISCUITS

When you haven't time to roll and cut, this is it.

All purpose flour	3 cups	750 mL
Granulated sugar	2 tbsp.	30 mL
Baking powder	5 tsp.	25 mL
Salt	1 tsp.	5 mL
Cold butter or margarine	½ cup	125 mL
Egg, beaten	1	1
Milk	1 cup	250 mL

In large bowl combine flour, sugar, baking powder and salt. Cut in butter until crumbly. Make a well in center.

In small bowl beat egg with spoon. Add milk. Pour into well. Stir lightly to mix. Batter should be sticky. If it isn't, stir in 1 tablespoon of milk at a time until it is. Drop by teaspoonful on ungreased baking sheet. Bake in 450°F (235°C) oven for 10-12 minutes or until browned. Better still, form into a circle to bake; break off a mound to eat. Serve hot with butter. Yield: 15-20 drops.

When Whistler saw his mother on her hands and knees scrubbing the floor he asked her if she was off her rocker.

Something so easy shouldn't be so good. A single recipe won't be enough.

All purpose flour	2 cups	500 mL
Granulated sugar	2 tbsp.	30 mL
Baking powder	4 tsp.	20 mL
Salt	1 tsp.	5 mL
Cold butter or margarine	¼ cup	50 mL
Cold milk	1 cup	250 mL
Butter or margarine, softened	⅓ cup	75 mL
Brown sugar, packed	1 cup	250 mL
Cinnamon	3 tsp.	15 mL
Currants or cut up raisins	⅓ cup	75 mL

In large bowl put flour, sugar, baking powder and salt. Cut in first amount of butter until crumbly. Make a well in center.

Pour milk into well. Stir to form soft dough adding a bit more milk if needed. Turn out on lightly floured surface. Knead 8-10 times. Roll into rectangle about ⅓ inch (1 cm) thick and 12 inches (30 cm) long. Width will vary.

Cream second amount of butter, brown sugar and cinnamon together well. Drop 1 measuring teaspoon (5 mL) into each of 12 greased muffin tins. Spread the remaining cinnamon mixture over dough rectangle. Sprinkle currants over top. Roll up as for jelly roll. Mark first then cut into 12 slices. Place cut side down in muffin pan. Bake in 400°F (200°C) oven for 20 to 25 minutes. Turn out on tray. Makes 12.

GLAZE: To ½ cup (125 mL) icing sugar, add enough milk or water to make a thin glaze. Drizzle over cinnamon rolls.

Pictured on page 53.

APPLE SCONES

Terrific aroma. Terrific taste. Perfect for tea time.

All purpose flour	2 cups	500 mL
Granulated sugar	¼ cup	50 mL
Baking powder	2 tsp.	10 mL
Baking soda	½ tsp.	2 mL
Salt	½ tsp.	2 mL
Cold butter or margarine	¼ cup	50 mL
Apple, peeled and grated	1	1
Milk	½ cup	125 mL

Milk for brushing tops
Sugar for sprinkling
Cinnamon for sprinkling.

Measure flour, sugar, baking powder, soda and salt into large bowl. Cut in butter until crumbly.

Add shredded apple and milk. Stir to form soft dough. Turn out on lightly floured surface. Knead gently 8-10 times. Pat into two 6 inch (15 cm) circles. Place on greased baking sheet. Brush tops with milk. Sprinkle with sugar then with cinnamon. Score each top into 6 pie shaped wedges. Bake in 425°F (220°C) oven for 15 minutes until browned and risen. Serve warm with butter. Yield: 12 scones.

CURRANT APPLE SCONES: Add ½ cup (125 mL) currants to batter.

Pictured on page 89.

1. Bran Scones page 102
2. Scottish Oat Scones page 92
3. Apple Scones page 88
4. Ginger Scones page 98

Rich little things that melt in your mouth.

All purpose flour	**2 cups**	**500 mL**
Butter or margarine	**1 cup**	**250 mL**
Egg yolk	**1**	**1**
Dairy sour cream	**¾ cup**	**175 mL**
Granulated sugar	**¼ cup**	**50 mL**
Cinnamon	**1 tsp.**	**5 mL**

Combine flour and butter in large bowl. Cut in butter until mixture is crumbly.

Beat egg yolk and sour cream together with spoon. Add to flour mixture. Mix together well. Chill covered in refrigerator at least 4 hours. If you make this in the evening, store overnight.

Stir sugar and cinnamon together to use instead of flour for rolling dough. Sprinkle some over working surface. Roll about ¼-⅓ of dough into circle about 10 inches (25 cm) in diameter sprinkling with sugar-cinnamon mixture on both sides as needed both to roll and for taste. Cut in 16 pie shape wedges. Beginning at outer wide edge, roll toward center. Arrange on ungreased baking sheet close together, not touching. Bake in 375°F (190°C) oven for 25 to 30 minutes until browned. Makes 4 dozen.

Pictured on page 53.

The firefly ran into a fan and was delighted.

SCOTTISH OAT SCONES

Nibble or lunch on it. It won't last for long.

All purpose flour	1½ cups	375 mL
Rolled oats	2 cups	500 mL
Granulated sugar	¼ cup	50 mL
Baking powder	4 tsp.	20 mL
Salt	½ tsp.	2 mL
Currants	½ cup	125 mL
Egg, beaten	1	1
Butter or margarine, melted	½ cup	125 mL
Milk	⅓ cup	75 mL

Put first six dry ingredients into large bowl. Mix. Make a well in center.

Beat egg until frothy. Mix in melted butter and milk. Pour into well. Stir to make soft dough. Pat into two 6 to 7 inch (15 to 18 cm) circles. Transfer to greased baking sheet. Score each top into 8 pie shaped wedges. Bake in 425°F (220°C) oven for 15 minutes until risen and browned. Split and butter. Yield: 16 scones.

Pictured on page 89.

A dog who attends a flea circus most likely will steal the whole show.

These perky little buns disappear in a flash.

All purpose flour	2 cups	500 mL
Granulated sugar	2 tbsp.	30 mL
Baking powder	3 tsp.	15 mL
Salt	½ tsp.	2 mL
Cold butter or margarine	½ cup	125 mL
Egg, beaten	1	1
Cold milk	½ cup	125 mL
Raspberry jam		

In large bowl put flour, sugar, baking powder, salt and butter. Cut in butter until crumbly. Make well in center.

Beat egg until light and frothy. Mix in milk. Pour all at once into well. Stir lightly to form soft dough. Add more milk if needed. On floured surface, knead dough 8-10 times. Pat or roll out to ¾ inch (2 cm) thickness. Using round cookie cutter, push straight down to cut. Arrange well apart on greased baking sheet. Make a deep hollow in top center of each biscuit. Drop small spoonful of jam into each hollow. Bake in 450°F (230°C) oven for 12-15 minutes. Serve hot. Makes 14-16.

Pictured on page 53.

If you pour hot water into a rabbit hole you get hot cross bunnies.

RICH TEA BISCUITS

Always a last minute favorite. So speedy to make. Fat content may be cut in half if desired for any of the following. Be sure to try them all.

All purpose flour	2 cups	500 mL
Granulated sugar	2 tbsp.	30 mL
Salt	1 tsp.	5 mL
Baking powder	4 tsp.	20 mL
Cream of tarter	½ tsp.	2 mL
Butter or margarine, cold	½ cup	125 mL
Cold milk	1 cup	250 mL

Put first five ingredients into bowl. Stir thoroughly.

Cut in butter until crumbly.

Pour in milk. Stir quickly to combine. Dough should be soft. Turn out on lightly floured surface. Knead gently 8-10 times. Roll or pat ½ to ¾ inch (2 cm) thick or half the thickness you want the baked product to be. Cut with small round cookie cutter. Place on greased cookie sheet close together for soft sides or apart for crisp sides. Bake in 450°F (230°C) oven for 12-15 minutes. Brushing biscuits with milk before baking will produce a pretty brown top. Makes 10.

Pictured on cover.

BISCUIT TOPPING: Place biscuits close together over hot casserole. Bake in 425°F (220°C) oven for 20-25 minutes. If casserole won't hold all of them, bake on separate pan.

BUTTERMILK BISCUITS: Reduce baking powder to 2 tsp. (10 mL), add ½ tsp. (2 mL) baking soda. Replace milk with buttermilk.

COCONUT ROLLS: Spread rolled rectangle of dough with a mixture of ⅓ cup (75 mL) brown sugar and ⅓ cup (75 mL) coconut. Roll and slice into 12 slices. Bake as for Rich Tea Biscuits.

(continued on next page)

Paré Pointer

The younger generation is the most creative so far. Ever watch one build a sandwich?

GRAHAM BISCUITS: Use ½ cup (125 mL) butter. Reduce flour to 1½ cups (375 mL). Add 1 cup (250 mL) graham cracker crumbs. A distinctive flavor.

ORANGE BISCUITS: Add 1 tbsp. (15 mL) grated orange rind. Substitute half orange juice for half of milk. Dip sugar cubes in some orange juice and press in top of each biscuit before baking.

PEANUT BUTTER BISCUITS: Reduce butter to ¼ cup (50 mL). Add ¼ cup (50 mL) peanut butter.

PIZZA CRUST: Make dough as above. Press or roll size of pizza pan. Proceed to make your favorite pizza.

TOMATO BISCUITS: Omit milk. Add ¾ cup (175 mL) tomato juice. Add ½ cup (125 mL) grated cheese (optional).

WHOLE WHEAT BISCUITS

A tender scrumptious biscuit.

All purpose flour	1 cup	250 mL
Whole wheat flour	1 cup	250 mL
Baking powder	4 tsp.	20 mL
Granulated sugar	1 tbsp.	15 mL
Salt	¾ tsp.	5 mL
Cold butter or margarine	4 tbsp.	50 mL
Milk	1 cup	250 mL

In mixing bowl put flours, baking powder, sugar and salt.

Add butter. Cut into dry ingredients until mixture is crumbly.

Add milk. Stir with fork until soft dough is formed. Turn out on lightly floured surface. Knead gently 8-10 times. Roll or pat dough ¾ inch (2 cm) thick. Cut with round 2 inch (5 cm) cookie cutter. If cut in squares or triangles, no re-rolling is necessary since no dough is left over. Arrange on ungreased baking sheet, close together for soft sides, 1 inch (2.5 cm) apart for crisp sides. Bake in 450°F (230°C) oven for 12-15 minutes until browned. Serve with butter. Yield: 10-12 biscuits.

Pictured on page 53.

SAVORY SAUSAGE BISCUITS

Serve this "meal in a biscuit" with soup. Excellent.

Sausage meat	½ lb.	250 g
All purpose flour	2 cups	500 mL
Baking powder	2 tsp.	10 mL
Baking soda	½ tsp.	3 mL
Salt	1 tsp.	5 mL
Butter or margarine	¼ cup	50 mL
Buttermilk	1 cup	250 mL

Brown sausage meat. Drain very well. Crumble. Set aside.

Put flour, baking powder, soda and salt in large bowl. Cut in butter until crumbly. Stir in sausage meat. Make a well in center.

Pour buttermilk into well. Stir quickly to form soft dough. Turn out on floured surface. Knead 8-10 times. Pat or roll ¾ inch (2 cm) thick. Cut into rounds, squares or triangles. Place on ungreased baking sheet. Bake in 450°F (235°C) oven for 12-15 minutes until browned. Makes 12-15 biscuits.

Pictured on page 125.

MAYONNAISE BISCUITS

So few ingredients. So easy.

All purpose flour	2 cups	500 mL
Baking powder	4 tsp.	20 mL
Salt	¾ tsp.	5 mL
Mayonnaise	¼ cup	75 mL
Milk	¾ cup	175 mL

Stir flour, baking powder and salt in bowl. Make a well in center.

Pour mayonnaise and milk into well. Stir to moisten until soft dough forms. Pat or roll on lightly floured surface. Cut into rounds. Place on ungreased baking sheet. Bake in 425°F (220°C) oven for 12 minutes or until brown. Yield: 12 biscuits.

Pictured on page 53.

Just right for a morning coffee party.

All purpose flour	2 cups	450 mL
Granulated sugar	¼ cup	50 mL
Baking powder	4 tsp.	20 mL
Salt	½ tsp.	2 mL
Cold butter or margarine	¼ cup	50 mL
Currants	½ cup	125 mL
Egg	1	1
Milk	⅔ cup	150 mL

Milk for brushing tops
Granulated sugar for sprinkling

In large bowl put flour, sugar, baking powder and salt. Add butter. Cut in until crumbly. Stir in currants. Make a well in center.

In small bowl, beat egg until frothy. Stir in milk. Pour into well. Stir with a fork to form soft dough. Turn out on lightly floured surface. Knead 8 to 10 times. Divide into two equal parts. Pat each into 6 inch (15 cm) circle. Transfer to greased baking sheet. Brush tops with milk and sprinkle with sugar. Score each top into 6 pie shaped markings. Bake in 425°F (220°C) oven for 15 minutes until risen and browned slightly. Serve hot with butter and jam. Yield: 12 scones.

BRAN CEREAL SCONES: Use only 1⅓ cups (325 mL) all purpose flour and add 1 cup (250 mL) bran flakes cereal.

CHEESE SCONES: Add 1 cup (250 mL) grated cheese.

FRUIT SCONES: Omit currants. Add 1 cup (250 mL) glazed fruit.

ORANGE SCONES: Add 1 tbsp. (15 mL) grated orange rind.

YOGURT SCONES: Omit milk. Add ¾ cup (175 mL) yogurt.

WHOLE WHEAT SCONES: Exchange half of the flour for whole wheat flour.

GINGER SCONES

Very tasty, dark and different, out of the ordinary.

All purpose flour	2 cups	500 mL
Granulated sugar	1 tbsp.	15 mL
Baking powder	2 tsp.	10 mL
Baking soda	½ tsp.	2 mL
Salt	¾ tsp.	5 mL
Cinnamon	½ tsp.	2 mL
Ginger	½ tsp.	2 mL
Cold butter or margarine	¼ cup	50 mL
Egg	1	1
Molasses	¼ cup	50 mL
Buttermilk or sour milk	½ cup	125 mL

Milk for brushing tops
Sugar for sprinkling

Measure first seven dry ingredients into large bowl. Add butter and cut in until crumbly. Make a well in center.

In small bowl beat egg until frothy. Mix in molasses and buttermilk. Stir with fork to make a soft dough. Turn out on lightly floured surface. Knead lightly 8-10 times. Divide into two parts. Pat each part into 6 inch (15 cm) circle. Place on greased baking sheet. Brush tops with milk. Sprinkle with sugar. Score each top into 6 pie shaped markings. Bake in 425°F (220°C) oven until risen and browned. Serve hot with lots of butter. Yield: 12 scones.

Pictured on page 89.

Note: Feel free to add raisins or currants.

Note: For sour milk add milk to 2 tsp. (10 mL) vinegar to measure ½ cup (125 mL).

BUTTERMILK SCONES: Omit cinnamon, ginger and molasses. use ⅔ cup (150 mL) buttermilk.

SOUR CREAM SCONES: Omit cinnamon, ginger and molasses. Use ¾ cup (175 mL) dairy sour cream instead of buttermilk.

So easy to make you can whip them up at a moment's notice.

All purpose flour	2 cups	500 mL
Granulated sugar	½ cup	125 mL
Baking powder	3 tsp.	15 mL
Salt	½ tsp.	2 mL
Cold butter or margarine	½ cup	125 mL
Egg	1	1
Milk	⅔ cup	150 mL

Milk for brushing tops
Sugar for sprinkling

Mix flour, sugar, baking powder and salt in large bowl. Cut in butter until crumbly.

Beat egg lightly in small bowl. Add milk. Pour into dry ingredients. Stir with fork to make a soft dough. Pat into two 6 inch (15 cm) rounds. Place on greased baking sheet. Brush tops with milk. Sprinkle with sugar. Score each top into 6 pie shaped wedges. Bake in 425°F (220°C) oven for 15 minutes until risen and golden brown. Split and butter. Yield: 12 scones.

CHELSEA BUNS

First prepare muffin cups. Grease bottoms of 12 cups thickly with butter or margarine. Sprinkle with brown sugar to make fairly thick layer. Sprinkle a few currants and chopped nuts into each cup.

Make a rich scone batter as above. Roll into square 9 × 9 inches (23 × 23 cm). Spread with following mixture.

Butter or margarine	⅓ cup	75 mL
Packed brown sugar	⅓ cup	75 mL
Raisins	½ cup	125 mL
Chopped nuts	½ cup	125 mL

Mix butter, sugar, raisins and nuts. Spread over rectangle. Roll as for jelly roll. Slice into 12 rounds. Put one in each cup. Bake in 450°F (230°C) oven for 12-15 minutes. Glaze when cool with ½ cup (125 mL) icing sugar mixed with enough water to make thin glaze.

TEA BUNS

Rich and raisiny. A snap to make.

All purpose flour	2 cups	500 mL
Granulated sugar	⅓ cup	75 mL
Baking powder	4 tsp.	20 mL
Salt	¾ tsp.	5 mL
Cold butter or margarine	½ cup	125 mL
Raisins	1 cup	250 mL
Egg	1	1
Milk	¾ cup	175 mL

Combine flour, sugar, baking powder and salt in large bowl. Cut in butter until crumbly. Stir in raisins. Make a well in center.

In another bowl beat egg slightly with spoon. Mix in milk. Pour into well. Stir to mix into a soft dough. Pat or roll out on lightly floured surface ¾ inch (2 cm) thick. Cut with biscuit cutter. Place on ungreased baking sheet. Bake in 400°F (200°C) oven for 20 minutes or until brown. Serve with butter. Makes 12-16.

Pictured on page 53.

There is no harm in always wishing for something you don't have. What else could you wish for?

Makes good use of extra cream you have on hand.

All purpose flour	4 cups	1 L
Granulated sugar	½ cup	125 mL
Baking powder	8 tsp.	40 mL
Salt	1 tsp.	5 mL
Beaten eggs	2	2
Heavy cream	1 cup	250 mL
Milk	1 cup	250 mL

Milk for brushing tops
Sugar for sprinkling

Combine flour, sugar, baking powder and salt. Stir.

In another bowl beat eggs until frothy. Add to flour mixture along with cream and milk. Stir until a soft ball of dough is formed. Turn out on lightly floured surface. Knead 8-10 times. Pat or roll 1 inch (2.5 cm) thick. Cut with round cookie cutter. Arrange on ungreased cookie sheet close together for soft sides and an inch (3 cm) apart for crisp sides. Brush tops with milk then sprinkle with sugar. Bake in 425°F (220°C) oven for 15 minutes until risen and browned. Yield: 2 dozen scones.

The girl vampire and the boy vampire were so sad. They loved in vein.

BRAN SCONES

Sugar adds to the flavor but can be omitted.

All purpose flour	1¾ cups	425 mL
Natural bran or all bran cereal	½ cup	125 mL
Granulated sugar	¼ cup	50 mL
Baking powder	3 tsp.	15 mL
Salt	1 tsp.	5 mL
Cold butter or margarine	¼ cup	50 mL
Egg	1	1
Milk	¾ cup	175 mL

Milk for brushing tops
Granulated sugar for sprinkling

Put flour, bran, sugar, baking powder and salt into large bowl. Cut in butter until crumbly.

In small bowl beat egg. Mix in milk. Pour into dry ingredients. Stir to make soft dough. Knead gently 8-10 times on lightly floured surface. Pat flat and cut in rounds or pat into two 6 inch (15 cm) circles. Place on greased baking sheet. Brush tops with milk and sprinkle with sugar. Score each top into 6 pie shaped wedges. Bake in 425°F (220°C) oven for 15 minutes until risen and browned. Yield: 12 scones.

Pictured on page 89.

Illegal and unlawful are two different things. The first is a sick bird, the second is against the law.

Greet your guests with the aroma of these scones fresh from the oven.

All purpose flour	1 cup	250 mL
Whole wheat flour	1 cup	250 mL
Granulated sugar	¼ cup	50 mL
Baking powder	4 tsp.	20 mL
Cinnamon	1½ tsp.	7 mL
Nutmeg	½ tsp.	3 mL
Salt	½ tsp.	2 mL
Cold butter or margarine	⅓ cup	75 mL
Raisins or currants	½ cup	125 mL
Eggs	1	1
Cold milk	⅔ cup	150 mL

Milk for brushing tops.
Granulated sugar for sprinkling.

Combine all first seven dry ingredients in large bowl. Cut in butter until crumbly. Stir in raisins. Make a well in center.

In small bowl beat egg until frothy. Mix in milk. Pour into well. Stir to make soft dough. Turn out on lightly floured surface. Knead gently 8-10 times. Pat into two 6 inch (15 cm) circles. Transfer to greased baking sheet. Brush tops with milk. Sprinkle with sugar. Score each top into 6 pie shaped wedges. Bake in 425°F (220°C) oven for 15 minutes until well risen and browned. Serve hot with butter. Maple butter goes well with this. Yield: 12 scones.

The only one to benefit from advice to sleep late would be a worm.

GRAHAM SCONES

Takes care of any appetite.

All purpose flour	1¼ cups	300 mL
Graham cracker crumbs	1 cup	250 mL
Rolled oats	½ cup	125 mL
Granulated sugar	¼ cup	50 mL
Baking powder	4 tsp.	20 mL
Salt	½ tsp.	2 mL
Shortening, butter or margarine	½ cup	125 mL
Currants	½ cup	125 mL
Egg	1	1
Cold milk	½ cup	125 mL

Milk for brushing tops
Sugar for sprinkling

Combine first six ingredients in bowl. Stir well.

Add shortening and cut in until crumbly.

Put egg into small bowl. Beat with fork. Mix in milk. Add to dry mixture. Stir with a fork until you can gather dough together in a ball. Turn onto lightly floured surface. Knead lightly 10 times. Form into two 6 inch (15 cm) circles. Brush with milk and sprinkle with sugar. Bake in 425°F (220°C) oven on a greased cookie sheet for 15 minutes. Cut in wedges. Serve warm with butter and your favorite jam. Yield: 12 scones.

When a kitten crawls into a photocopier it comes out a copycat.

GRAHAM TEA BISCUITS

Very good. These have a distinctive flavor.

All purpose flour	1½ cups	375 mL
Graham cracker crumbs	1 cup	250 mL
Granulated sugar	2 tbsp.	30 mL
Baking powder	4 tsp.	20 mL
Salt	½ tsp.	2 mL
Butter or margarine, cold	½ cup	125 mL
Milk	¾ cup	175 mL

Mix flour, cracker crumbs, sugar, baking powder and salt together. Cut in shortening until crumbly.

Add milk. Stir with fork to make soft ball. Add more milk if needed. Turn out on lightly floured surface. Knead lightly with hands ten times. Roll or pat out ¾ inch (2 cm) thick. Using small round cookie cutter, cut out biscuits. Arrange on ungreased baking sheet. Bake in 425°F (220°C) oven for 10-12 minutes. Makes 12.

Trains that are simply never on time still need timetables. Otherwise how would you know if they are early or late?

CROUTONS

Such a bargain to make your own. Nothing to it.

Stale bread
Melted butter or margarine

Remove crusts from stale bread slices. Brush bread with melted butter or margarine. Cut in small cubes. Arrange on ungreased baking sheet. Bake in 350°F (180°C) oven for about 15 minutes until browned. Cool. Store in covered container or plastic bag. Serve in soup or salad.

GARLIC CROUTONS: After brushing bread with melted butter, sprinkle with garlic salt. Proceed as above.

CINNAMON TOAST

A Sunday night tradition with our family.

Butter or margarine	1 cup	250 mL
Packed brown sugar	2½ cups	625 mL
Cinnamon	2½ tbsp.	40 mL

Have butter soft. Mix all together well until spreadable. Resist the urge to add more butter. It would be easier to spread but makes the flavor too bland. Store in covered container in refrigerator if you used butter, on kitchen shelf if you used margarine.

Spread on hot toast as desired.

1. Cheese Loaf page 112
2. Boston Brown Bread page 115
3. Boston Banner Bread page 114
4. Savory Onion Bread page 116

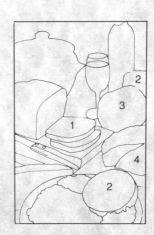

CINNAMON BREAD

As tasty and aromatic as can be! Good bread! Rich enough for lunch.

All purpose flour	2 cups	500 mL
Granulated sugar	1 cup	250 mL
Baking powder	2 tsp.	10 mL
Baking soda	½ tsp.	2 mL
Cinnamon	1½ tsp.	10 mL
Salt	1 tsp.	5 mL
Sour milk or buttermilk	1 cup	250 mL
Cooking oil	¼ cup	50 mL
Eggs	2	2
Vanilla	2 tsp.	10 mL

Measure all ingredients in order given into large mixing bowl. Beat 3 minutes. Pour into a greased loaf pan 9 × 5 × 3 inch (23 × 12 × 7 cm). Smooth top. Sprinkle with topping.

TOPPING:

Granulated sugar	2 tbsp.	30 mL
Cinnamon	1 tsp.	5 mL
Margarine or butter	2 tsp.	10 mL

Combine all ingredients, mixing until crumbly. Sprinkle over smoothed batter. Using knife, cut in a light swirling motion to give a marbled effect. Bake in 350°F (180°C) oven for about 50 minutes. Test with toothpick. When inserted it should come out clean. Remove from pan to rack to cool. Yield: 1 loaf.

Note: To make sour milk, add milk to 1 tbsp. (15 mL) vinegar to measure 1 cup (250 mL).

BANNOCK — OFF THE TRAIL

A few extras added to make an excellent variation.

All purpose flour	2½ cups	625 mL
Granulated sugar	3 tbsp.	50 mL
Baking powder	2 tbsp.	30 mL
Salt	1 tsp.	5 mL
Butter or margarine or lard	2 tbsp.	30 mL
Mashed potatoes	1 cup	250 mL
Milk	1 cup	250 mL

In large bowl, combine flour, sugar, baking powder and salt. Add butter. Cut in until it is in tiny pieces.

Add potatoes. Cut and stir in potatoes.

Pour in milk. Stir with fork to form ball. Turn out on working surface. Knead about 10 times. Place on ungreased cookie sheet. Pat down to ¾ to 1 inch (2 to 2.5 cm) thick. Bake in 400°F (200°C) for about 20 minutes or until well browned. Yield: 1 round.

Variation: Omit sugar. Add 2 tbsp. (30 mL) molasses.

WHOLE WHEAT BREAD

This is the best tasting, best looking loaf you could wish for to grace your table. It is moist and a rich brown color. Good with any meal.

Whole wheat flour	2 cups	500 mL
All purpose flour	1 cup	250 mL
Granulated sugar	¼ cup	50 mL
Baking powder	2 tsp.	10 mL
Baking soda	1 tsp.	5 mL
Salt	1 tsp.	5 mL
Buttermilk or sour milk	1½ cups	375 mL
Molasses	¼ cup	50 mL
Cooking oil	¼ cup	50 mL

(continued on next page)

In large bowl combine all six dry ingredients. Stir to combine thoroughly. Make a well in the center.

In a small bowl put buttermilk, molasses and oil. Stir until molasses has thinned and mixed in. Pour into well. Stir just enough to combine. Turn into greased loaf pan 9 × 5 × 3 inch (23 × 12 × 7 cm). Bake in 350°F (180°C) oven for 40-50 minutes. Remove from pan to cool. Serve with butter. Yield: 1 loaf.

GRAHAM BREAD: Use graham flour instead of whole wheat.

Note: To make sour milk add milk to 1½ tablespoons (25 mL) vinegar to measure 1½ cups (375 mL).

RYE BREAD

Especially good with a corned beef meal.

Rye flour	2 cups	500 mL
All purpose flour	1½ cups	375 mL
Packed brown sugar	¼ cup	50 mL
Baking soda	1½ tsp.	7 mL
Baking powder	1 tsp.	5 mL
Salt	½ tsp.	2 mL
Buttermilk	1¾ cups	425 mL
Cooking oil	2 tbsp.	30 mL

Measure all six dry ingredients together in large bowl. Stir thoroughly. Make a well in the center.

Add buttermilk and oil. Stir just to moisten. Turn into greased loaf pan 9 × 5 × 3 inches (23 × 12 × 7 cm). Bake in 350°F (180°C) oven for 1 hour. Remove from pan to cool. Serve with butter. Yield: 1 loaf.

CARAWAY RYE BREAD: Add 1 tablespoon (15 mL) caraway seeds.

RAISIN BREAD

Out of bread? This cinnamon flavored bread fills the bill. Good toasted too.

All purpose flour	3 cups	750 mL
Granulated sugar	½ cup	125 mL
Baking powder	3 tsp.	15 mL
Baking soda	½ tsp.	2 mL
Salt	1 tsp.	5 mL
Cinnamon	¾ tsp.	5 mL
Raisins	1 cup	250 mL
Egg, beaten	1	1
Melted butter or margarine	¼ cup	50 mL
Milk	1 cup	250 mL

In large bowl measure all seven dry ingredients. Stir thoroughly. Make a well in center.

In small bowl beat egg until frothy. Mix in melted butter and milk. Pour into well. Stir just enough to moisten. Scrape into greased loaf pan 9 × 5 × 3 inch (23 × 12 × 7 cm). Bake in 350°F (180°C) oven for 1 hour. Serve plain or toasted with butter. Yield: 1 loaf.

CHEESE LOAF

Moist, delicious and attractive. A good bread substitute. And so simple to make.

All purpose flour	3 cups	750 mL
Baking powder	4 tsp.	20 mL
Salt	½ tsp.	3 mL
Grated medium or sharp cheese	1½ cups	375 mL
Milk	1½ cups	375 mL
Melted butter or margarine	2 tbsp.	30 mL

Combine flour, baking powder, salt and cheese in large bowl. Stir thoroughly.

Add milk and melted butter. Stir to form soft dough. Put in greased loaf pan 9 × 5 × 3 inch (23 × 12 × 7 cm). Bake in 400°F (200°C) oven for 35-40 minutes. Remove from pan to cool. Serve with butter. Yield: 1 loaf.

Pictured on page 107.

IRISH SODA BREAD

A quick version of this well known bread.

All purpose flour	4 cups	1 L
Granulated sugar	2 tbsp.	30 mL
Baking powder	1 tbsp.	15 mL
Baking soda	1 tsp.	5 mL
Salt	1 tsp.	5 mL
Cold butter or margarine	6 tbsp.	100 mL
Buttermilk	2 cups	500 mL

In mixing bowl combine flour, sugar, baking powder, soda and salt. Stir thoroughly. Cut in butter until crumbly.

Add buttermilk. Stir just enough to moisten. Turn out on lightly floured surface. Knead 8-10 times. Put in greased loaf pan 9 × 5 × 3 inch (23 × 12 × 7 cm). Bake in 350°F (180°C) oven for 1 hour until browned and inserted toothpick comes out clean. This may also be baked in a casserole or on a baking sheet. Yield: 1 loaf.

Variation: Add 1 cup currants or raisins.

JOHNNY CAKE

Double flavor. Corn and corn. Good eating corn bread.

Corn meal, yellow or white	1 cup	250 mL
Baking powder	1 tsp.	5 mL
Baking soda	½ tsp.	2 mL
Salt	½ tsp.	2 mL
Eggs	2	2
Cream style corn	1 cup	250 mL
Cooking oil	¼ cup	50 mL
Dairy sour cream	1 cup	250 mL

Stir together meal, baking powder, soda and salt.

Add eggs and mix together. Stir in corn, oil and sour cream. Pour into greased 8 × 8 inch (20 × 20 cm) cake pan. Bake in 400°F (200°C) oven for 25 minutes or until browned. Serve with butter.

BOSTON BANNER BREAD

The best! Would you serve baked beans without it?

Whole wheat flour	1 cup	250 mL
Cornmeal	1 cup	250 mL
Graham cracker crumbs	1¼ cups	300 mL
Granulated sugar	¼ cup	50 mL
Baking soda	1 tsp.	5 mL
Salt	½ tsp.	2 mL
Buttermilk	1¼ cups	300 mL
Molasses	½ cup	125 mL
Vegetable oil	¼ cup	50 mL

Combine all dry ingredients in bowl. Stir well.

Pour buttermilk, molasses and cooking oil into small bowl. Blend together. Pour into dry mixture. Stir to combine. Divide between two greased 28 ounce (796 mL) cans or three greased 19 ounce (540 mL) cans. Cover tops with foil held in place with string or elastic. Set on rack in large pot. (Metal jar rings work well.) Fill pot with boiling water until it reaches at least half way up the cans. Cover pot. Keep water boiling gently, adding more as needed to keep level up. Steam for 1½ hours until an inserted toothpick comes out clean. Cool for 10 minutes, then remove from cans. Serve with butter with or without baked beans. Yield: 2 or 3 loaves.

Variation: Add 1 cup (250 mL) seeded raisins.

Pictured on page 107.

IRISH BROWN BREAD

A healthy brown bread for a meal. So easy to make. Try it toasted.

All purpose flour	2 cups	500 mL
Whole wheat flour	1½ cups	375 mL
Natural bran	½ cup	125 mL
Granulated sugar	¼ cup	50 mL
Baking soda	1½ tsp.	10 mL
Salt	1½ tsp.	10 mL
Buttermilk or sour milk	2 cups	500 mL
Cooking oil	¼ cup	50 mL

(continued on next page)

In large bowl measure in flours, bran, sugar, baking soda and salt. Mix together and make a well in center.

Pour in buttermilk and oil. Stir just to moisten. Scrape into greased loaf pan 9 × 5 × 3 (23 × 12 × 7 cm). Bake in 350°F (180°C) oven for 1 hour. Remove from pan to cool. Serve plain or toasted, both with butter. Yield: 1 loaf.

IRISH RAISIN BREAD: Add 1 cup (250 mL) raisins.

Note: For sour milk add milk to 2 tablespoons (30 mL) vinegar to measure 2 cups (500 mL).

BOSTON BROWN BREAD

Bake some beans to complete the meal.

Whole wheat flour	1 cup	250 mL
Cornmeal	1 cup	250 mL
All purpose flour	1 cup	250 mL
Brown sugar	2 tbsp.	30 mL
Baking powder	1 tsp.	7 mL
Baking soda	1 tsp.	5 mL
Salt	1 tsp.	5 mL
Raisins (optional)	1 cup	250 mL
Water	1¼ cups	300 mL
Molasses	¾ cup	175 mL
Cooking oil	2 tbsp.	30 mL

Combine all seven dry ingredients in large bowl. Add raisins if you are going to use them. Stir to blend thoroughly. Make a well in center.

In small bowl stir water and molasses until blended. Add oil and pour into well. Stir just to moisten. Batter will be lumpy. Fill two greased 28 oz. (796 mL) or three 19 oz. (540 mL) tins ⅔ full. Cover with foil and secure with string. Place tins on rack in pan with boiling water halfway up the sides of tins. Cover pan. Steam for 2 hours. Add more boiling water as needed to keep water half way up tins. Remove from tins. Serve hot or cold. Makes 2 or 3 loaves.

Pictured on page 107.

SAVORY ONION BREAD

Looks great. Tastes great. Goes well with green salads.

All purpose flour	1½ cups	375 mL
Baking powder	3 tsp.	15 mL
Salt	1 tsp.	5 mL
Cold butter or margarine	2 tbsp.	30 mL
Grated sharp cheddar cheese	½ cup	125 mL
Finely chopped onion	½ cup	125 mL
Butter or margarine	1 tbsp.	15 mL
Egg, slightly beaten	1	1
Milk	½ cup	125 mL
Grated sharp cheddar cheese	½ cup	125 mL

Combine flour, baking powder and salt in large bowl. Cut in butter until crumbly. Stir in cheese. Make a well in center.

Fry onion in butter slowly until clear and golden. Set aside.

Beat egg with spoon in small bowl. Stir in milk. Add onion. Pour into well. Stir to moisten and form a soft dough. Pat into greased 8 inch (20 cm) round or square pan.

Sprinkle cheese over top. Bake in 400°F (200°C) oven for 25 minutes. Serve hot to 6 medium appetites.

Pictured on page 107.

He wanted the doctor to treat him but he had to pay just like the rest of us.

Fluffy moist dumplings are always a treat.

All purpose flour	1 cup	250 mL
Baking powder	2 tsp.	10 mL
Granulated sugar	1 tsp.	5 mL
Salt	½ tsp.	2 mL
Butter or margarine	1 tbsp.	15 mL
Milk	½ cup	125 mL

Stir flour, baking powder, sugar and salt together in medium size bowl. Cut in butter until crumbly. Stir in milk to make soft dough. Drop by spoonfuls onto boiling stew. Cover and simmer 15 minutes without lifting lid. Serve. Makes 6 dumplings.

PARSLEY DUMPLINGS: Add 1 tablespoon (15 mL) parsley flakes.

GRAHAM CORNBREAD

The best cornbread going. Extra flavor.

Buttermilk	¾ cup	175 mL
Yellow cornmeal	1 cup	250 mL
Butter or margarine	½ cup	125 mL
Granulated sugar	½ cup	125 mL
Egg	1	1
Graham cracker crumbs	1 cup	250 mL
All purpose flour	½ cup	125 mL
Baking powder	1 tsp.	5 mL
Baking soda	1 tsp.	5 mL
Salt	½ tsp.	2 mL
Buttermilk	1 cup	250 mL

Combine buttermilk and cornmeal in small bowl. Set aside.

In mixing bowl beat butter, sugar and egg together well.

Stir crumbs, flour, baking powder, soda and salt together to mix well. Add alternately with the last 1 cup buttermilk. Stir in cornmeal mixture. Turn into greased 8 × 8 inch (20 × 20 cm) pan. Bake in 350°F (180°C) oven for 45 minutes. An inserted toothpick will come out clean. Serve with meal in place of bread, or serve with butter and maple syrup.

CREAM PUFFS

This easy to make puff doubles as a dessert or as a luncheon helper.

Boiling water	1 cup	250 mL
Butter or margarine	½ cup	125 mL
Salt	¼ tsp.	1 mL
All purpose flour	1 cup	250 mL
Eggs	4	4

Put boiling water, butter and salt in medium size saucepan over low heat. Stir to melt butter.

Add flour all at once. Stir vigorously until it forms a ball and pulls away from sides of pan. Remove from heat.

Add eggs one at a time beating thoroughly after each is added. Drop by spoonfuls onto greased baking sheet leaving room for expansion. Bake in 425°F (220°C) oven for 30 minutes. They should look dry with no beads of moisture showing. When cool, cut top almost off, fill with flavored whipped cream or creamed meat. Sprinkle tops with icing sugar. Makes 12 large cream puffs. For 2-3 dozen smaller puffs bake shorter time.

DEEP FRIED CREAM PUFFS: Make batter as above. Drop by spoonful into deep frying fat 375°F (190°C) and cook for 12-15 minutes until golden, turning frequently. Drain on paper towels. When cool, cut off tops. Fill with cold or hot mixtures of your choice. Replace tops. Very crisp and tender. Excellent.

Pictured on page 71.

BANNOCK — ON THE TRAIL

Years ago, anyone "on the trail" had these few staples with them.

All purpose flour	3 cups	750 mL
Salt	1 tsp.	5 mL
Baking powder	2 tbsp.	30 mL
Butter or margarine, melted	¼ cup	50 mL
Water	1½ cups	375 mL

(continued on next page)

Measure flour, salt and baking powder into large bowl. Stir to mix.

Pour melted butter and water over flour mixture. Stir with fork to make a ball. Turn out on working surface. Knead gently about 10 times. Pat into a flat circle ¾ to 1 inch (2 cm) thick. Cook in greased frying pan over medium heat allowing about 15 minutes each side. Use two lifters for easy turning. Serve hot with butter. Break off chunks or slice with knife. May also be baked on greased baking sheet in 350°F (180°C) oven for 25-30 minutes.

Note: Bacon or beef drippings may be used instead of butter.

YORKSHIRE PUDDING

Traditional accompaniment to roast beef and gravy.

Eggs, room temperature	2	2
Milk, room temperature	1 cup	250 mL
All purpose flour	⅞ cup	225 mL
Salt	½ tsp.	2 mL
Beef drippings	¼ cup	50 mL

Beat eggs in medium bowl until frothy. Mix in milk. Gradually beat in flour and salt, beating until smooth and bubbly.

Heat beef drippings in 8 × 8 inch (20 × 20 cm) pan, or divide among 12 muffin cups. When sizzling hot, pour batter into pan, or pour into muffin cups ½ full. Bake in 450°F (230°C) oven for about 30 minutes for muffin cups and longer for pan. It should be puffed and browned. Serves 6-8.

Whenever you find someone who is convinced he is a real wit, give him the benefit of the doubt. He is probably half right.

POPOVERS

May be served with butter and jam or honey. Will collapse if under-baked.

Eggs	2	2
Milk	1 cup	250 mL
Melted butter or margarine	3 tbsp.	45 mL
All purpose flour	1 cup	250 mL
Salt	½ tsp.	2 mL

Beat eggs until frothy. Mix in milk and butter. Add flour and salt gradually, beating until smooth. Spoon into greased muffin tins filling ½ full. Bake in 450°F (230°C) oven for about 30 minutes until puffed and brown. Serve at once. Do not freeze. Makes 9.

BOILED BAGEL

Makes a nice change to serve with salad, soup or any meal.

Frozen bread dough (loaf)	1	1
Boiling water	2-3 qts.	2-3 L
Salt	1 tbsp.	15 mL
Granulated sugar	1 tbsp.	15 mL
Sesame seeds		
Poppy seeds		

Thaw loaf of bread in refrigerator overnight, being sure to remove from wrapper and put in plastic bag first. In morning cut loaf into 10 to 12 pieces. On floured surface, stretch and shape each piece into shape of bagel, like a ring.

In fairly large pot put water, salt and sugar. Drop 3 or 4 bagels into boiling water. When they rise to the top, remove from water to towel to drain. When all are boiled and drained, arrange on greased baking sheet. Sprinkle with sesame or poppy seeds or leave plain. Bake in 375°F (190°C) oven for 10 minutes or until golden brown. Yield: 1 dozen bagels.

Try them all both as a loaf and as toasted slices.

Slice a French loaf in thick slices. If you are going to wrap in foil, cut slices all the way through. If you are going to heat loaf in oven un-wrapped, cut slices almost to the bottom but not through it. Have butter or margarine at room temperature before beginning. Mix the ingre-dients of your favorite spread together and spread on both sides of cut slices. Reshape into loaf. Wrap in foil. Heat in 350°F (180°C) oven for 20 minutes. Or spread mixture on top of thick slices to broil in oven. Watch carefully as they burn easily. Before broiling, bread slices can be but-tered then sprinkled with flavoring ingredient. Saves time when time is at a premium.

CELERY BREAD

Butter or margarine	½ cup	125 mL
Celery salt	½ tsp.	3 mL

CHEESE BREAD

Shredded cheddar cheese	⅓ cup	75 mL
Butter or margarine	⅓ cup	75 mL
Mayonnaise	1 tbsp.	15 mL

CURRIED BREAD

Butter or margarine	½ cup	125 mL
Curry powder	½ tsp.	3 mL

GARLIC BREAD

Butter or margarine	½ cup	125 mL
Garlic salt	½ tsp.	3 mL

HERB BREAD

Butter or margarine	½ cup	125 mL
Thyme	⅛ tsp.	0.5 mL
Marjoram	⅛ tsp.	0.5 mL
Rosemary	⅛ tsp.	0.5 mL
Garlic powder	⅛ tsp.	0.5 mL

ONION BREAD

Butter or margarine	½ cup	125 mL
Onion salt	½ tsp.	3 mL

PARMESAN BREAD

Grated parmesan cheese	¼ cup	50 mL
Butter or margarine	½ cup	125 mL

DANISH FLATBREAD

This is easy enough for any cook. Easier to eat.

Rolled oats, ground	3 cups	750 mL
All purpose flour	1½ cups	375 mL
Baking soda	1 tsp.	5 mL
Salt	1 tsp.	5 mL
Buttermilk	1¼ cups	300 mL
Butter or margarine, melted	½ cup	125 mL

Grind oats in blender or food chopper until crumbly. Measure all ingre-dients into large bowl. Mix together well to form stiff dough. Let rest 20 minutes. Divide into 8 equal ball shape pieces. Roll on lightly floured surface as thin as possible. Fry on hot greased skillet 350°F (180°C) turning to cook other side. When brown spots appear, it is ready. Serve either hot or cold buttered with choice of jams, syrups, or honey. Yield: 8 sheets.

FLATBREAD

A crisp flatbread of Norwegian origin, Anna's best.

All purpose flour	2 cups	500 mL
Whole wheat flour	2 cups	500 mL
Natural bran	2 cups	500 mL
Granulated sugar	¼ cup	50 mL
Salt	3 tsp.	15 mL
Baking powder	2 tsp.	10 mL
Baking soda	1 tsp.	5 mL
Hot water	1 cup	250 mL
Buttermilk	1 cup	250 mL
Butter or margarine, melted	¾ cup	175 mL

Mix all seven dry ingredients together in a large bowl.

Add water, buttermilk and melted butter. Stir quickly just to moisten. Make into balls the size of an egg. Roll with lefse rolling pin (or your own) until paper thin. Use flour, enough to keep from sticking. Bake on large grill or electric frying pan at 400°F (200°C) until each side is browned. Dry in 300°F (150°C) oven 3-5 minutes. Should be dry and crisp. Break into pieces to serve. Yield: 2 dozen sheets.

Try this flat bread from India. It doesn't take long to make.

Whole wheat flour	2 cups	500 mL
Salt	½ tsp.	2 mL
Water to start	¾ cup	175 mL
Melted butter		

Mix flour, salt and water in bowl to form stiff dough. Add more water, a little at a time, if needed. Let rest for 30 minutes. Roll egg size pieces very thin. Fry on hot griddle or pan 400°F (200°C). Drops of water really bounce in a hurry when pan is hot enough. Cook until brown spots appear. Brush with melted butter and serve. Keep in towel if needed to be kept warm. Makes 10 circles about 7 inches (18 cm) in diameter.

For a favorite Indian bread this is it. Deep fried flat bread.

Whole wheat flour	2 cups	500 mL
Baking powder	2 tsp.	10 mL
Salt	½ tsp.	2 mL
Melted butter or margarine	1 tbsp.	15 mL
Water	¾-1 cup	200-250 mL

Mix all together in medium size bowl adding more water if needed to make a stiff dough. Turn out on floured surface. Knead 12 times. Roll small egg sized pieces very thin, ⅛ inch (½ cm) thick. Melt lard or oil 1½ inch (4 cm) deep in large skillet or wok. Heat to 375°F (190°C). Drop in one sheet at a time. Press down with large spoon. Turn over once. Cook until light brown. Drain on paper towels. Serve hot. Makes 14 circles.

CHEESE STRAWS

These are good and very delicate.

All purpose flour	2 cups	500 mL
Grated sharp cheddar cheese	2 cups	500 mL
Butter or margarine	¾ cup	175 mL
Baking powder	1 tsp.	5 mL
Cayenne pepper	¼ tsp.	1 mL
Salt	½ tsp.	2 mL

Measure all ingredients into large bowl. Mix together well. Roll pieces of dough into thicker than pencil shaped sticks. Cut into 4-5 inch (10-12 cm) lengths. Bake in 400°F (200°C) oven for 5 minutes or until browned. Makes 4 dozen.

Pictured on page 53.

This crisp, nutty flavored flatbread can be served with soup or just as a snack.

Egg, beaten	1	1
Cooking oil	1 tbsp.	15 mL
Milk	⅔ cup	150 mL
All purpose flour	2⅔ cups	600 mL
Salt	1½ tsp.	7 mL
Granulated sugar	2 tsp.	10 mL
Sesame seeds	2 tbsp.	30 mL

Beat egg until frothy. Add remaining ingredients. Mix together well. Dough will be stiff. Let stand 30 minutes. Divide dough into 6 pieces. Roll out very thinly — as thinly as you can and still be able to handle it. Bake on ungreased cooking sheet. Bake on rack in top third part of 375°F (190°C) oven for 15 minutes until browned. Put cake pan containing some water on lower rack for moisture the first 5 minutes and remove water for the remainder. Break in chunks to store in plastic bag when cool. Sesame seeds may be sprinkled over top of dough during last part of rolling rather than added to dough during mixing if you find it easier. They tend to drop out when dough is being handled. Yield: 6 sheets.

Pictured on page 53.

A man who doesn't marry is a real sharpshooter. He never Mrs.

LEFSE

A soft Norwegian flatbread, a favorite from Agnes.

Mashed potato	**6 cups**	**1.5 L**
Butter or margarine, softened	**3 tbsp.**	**50 mL**
Salt	**1 tsp.**	**5 mL**
Light cream or milk	**½ cup**	**125 mL**
All purpose flour	**3 cups**	**750 mL**

Measure all ingredients into large bowl. Mix together. Make a ball into the shape of a Japanese orange. Roll with a lefse rolling pin (or your own) on a lightly floured surface or on a lightly floured tea towel. Roll as thin as possible to still be handled. Fry on griddle 400°F (200°C) turning once. For turning use spatula or clean, flat stick. When brown spots appear they are cooked. Yield: 24 sheets.

Serving Suggestions:

1. Butter as for bread.

2. Spread butter over lefse. Sprinkle with granulated sugar. Roll from each of two sides to center. Cut down center between rolls. Cut each roll into 2½ inch (6 cm) lengths.

3. Cinnamon may be sprinkled over butter and sugar as in No. 2. Roll and cut as directed.

4. Mix equal parts butter and sour cream blended together. Spread on one half of lefse. Sprinkle with granulated sugar. Fold other half over. Cut in wedges. Keep in cloth in plastic bag until needed.

A dancer goes quick on her beautiful legs. A duck goes quack on her beautiful eggs.

CHEESE CRACKERS

With different toppings you get four kinds of crackers in one baking.

Grated sharp cheddar cheese	**2 cups**	**500 mL**
All purpose flour	**2 cups**	**500 mL**
Butter or margarine	**½ cup**	**125 mL**
Salt	**1 tsp.**	**5 mL**
Paprika	**¼ tsp.**	**2 mL**
Cayenne pepper	**¼ tsp.**	**2 mL**
Water	**½ cup**	**125 mL**

Mix all together in bowl. Shape into rolls 1½ inch (4 cm) wide. Chill at least 2 hours wrapped in wax paper. Cut in thin slices and place on ungreased baking sheet. Sprinkle with coarse salt. Press gently. Bake in 425°F (220°C) oven for 5 minutes or until browned. Makes 4 dozen.

These can also be rolled out on a floured surface and cut. Optional toppings are: brush with water then sprinkle with garlic salt, celery salt or curry powder.

Pictured on page 53.

Don't look for oysters in oyster soup. Would you expect angels to be in an angel cake?

SODA CRACKERS

A cookie-like cracker. Use with your favorite cheese.

All purpose flour	2 cups	500 mL
Granulated sugar	½ cup	125 mL
Cold butter or margarine	¼ cup	50 mL
Egg, beaten	1	1
Baking soda	¾ tsp.	5 mL
Water	2 tsp.	13 mL

Put flour and sugar in bowl. Cut in butter until crumbly. Make a well in center.

Beat egg until frothy. Dissolve soda in water in small container and add to egg. Pour into well. Stir to make firm batter. If too stiff, add water, only one small spoonful at a time. Roll thin on lightly floured surface. Cut into rounds or squares. Pierce with fork. Bake on greased baking sheet in 350°F (180°C) oven for about 15 minutes or until golden color. Makes 5-6 dozen small crackers.

SESAME CRACKERS: Brush with fork beaten egg white. Sprinkle with sesame seeds before baking.

SALTED CRACKERS: Brush with melted butter and sprinkle with salt before baking.

Pictured on page 53.

GRAHAM CRACKERS

Use whole or make into crumbs to use with recipes from the cook book "Company's Coming — Squares".

All purpose flour	2 cups	500 mL
Graham flour	¼ cup	125 mL
Packed brown sugar	½ cup	125 mL
Baking soda	1 tsp.	5 mL
Salt	1 tsp.	5 mL
Butter or margarine, softened	½ cup	125 mL
Cooking oil	¼ cup	50 mL
Water	¼ cup	60 mL

Measure all ingredients into large bowl. Mix together well. Divide dough in half. Roll out half of dough directly on cookie sheet. It crumbles too much to transfer from one surface to another. If yours has sides turn upside down and use the bottom. Roll 12 × 10 inches (30 × 25 cm). Dust rolling pin with flour as needed. Use ruler to guide knife across dough to lightly score every 2 inches (5 cm). Prick with a fork trying to keep holes in line for an even professional look. Bake in 425°F (220°C) oven for about 10 minutes or until browned. These crisp as they cool. Cut on lines while hot for a clean edge. Yield: 5 dozen small wafers.

Note: Dough can be chilled in rolls then sliced and baked.

The dirty crooks. They stole everything but the soap and towels.

SESAME STICKS

These tasty sticks are simple to make. Useful for snacks.

Eggs	3	3
Granulated sugar	1 tbsp.	15 mL
Cooking oil	½ cup	125 mL
All purpose flour	1¼ cups	300 mL
Salt	½ tsp.	2 mL
Sesame seeds		

Beat eggs in mixing bowl until light colored and thick. Add sugar and oil. Beat very well.

Stir flour and salt together. Add 1 tablespoon at a time as you continue beating. Roll small ball of dough into shape of a thick pencil 6 inches (15 cm) long. Roll in sesame seeds. Arrange on ungreased pans. Bake in 350°F (180°C) oven for 25-30 minutes until brown and crisp. Makes 2 dozen.

Note: If you want more seeds to stick try brushing first with slightly beaten egg white. It acts like glue.

Pictured on page 53.

WHOLE WHEAT CRACKERS

Just what the party needs — a healthy cracker.

All purpose flour	1 cup	250 mL
Whole wheat flour	1 cup	250 mL
Granulated sugar	2 tbsp.	30 mL
Salt	¾ tsp.	5 mL
Baking soda	1 tsp.	5 mL
Butter or margarine, softened	½ cup	125 mL
Water	¾ cup	175 mL

Measure all ingredients into bowl. Mix together well. Roll half of dough out direcly onto cookie sheet. Roll thin. Cut into squares by using ruler to guide knife. Dust rolling pin with flour as needed. Prick with a fork keeping holes evenly placed. Brush lightly with water. Sprinkle with salt. Bake in 425°F (220°C) oven for about 10 minutes until browned. Yield: 5 dozen crackers.

So easy to whip up from scratch. Can be increased quickly for extra plates.

All purpose flour	1½ cups	325 mL
Granulated sugar	1 tbsp.	15 mL
Baking powder	1 tbsp.	15 mL
Salt	½ tsp.	2 mL
Egg, beaten	1	1
Cooking oil	2 tbsp.	30 mL
Milk	1½ cups	375 mL

Combine flour, sugar, baking powder and salt in medium size bowl.

Beat egg slightly in small bowl. Mix in oil and milk. Add to dry ingredients. Stir. A few small lumps in batter are preferable. Add more or less milk to have thicker or thinner pancakes. Pan is ready when drops of water bounce all over it. Drop batter by spoonful onto lightly greased hot pan 380°F (190°C). When bubbles appear and edges begin to dry, turn to brown other side. Serve hot with butter and maple syrup. Makes 12.

GRAHAM PANCAKES: Use 1¼ cups (300 mL) flour and add ½ cup (125 mL) graham cracker crumbs.

BLUEBERRY PANCAKES: Fold in ¾-1 cup (175-250 mL) blueberries.

WHEAT GERM PANCAKES: Add ½ cup (125 mL) wheat germ plus ¼ cup (50 mL) more milk to batter.

MAPLE SYRUP

Make your own. It's so easy and fast.

Packed brown sugar	2 cups	500 mL
Water	1 cup	250 mL
Maple flavoring	1 tsp.	5 mL

In medium saucepan combine sugar and water. Bring to boil stirring frequently. Remove from heat and add flavoring. Serve with pancakes, waffles and French toast. Makes 2 cups.

CRÊPES

Can be cooked ahead and frozen until required.

Eggs	4	4
Milk	1 cup	250 mL
Water	1 cup	250 mL
All purpose flour	2 cups	500 mL
Cooking oil	4 tbsp.	50 mL
Salt	¼ tsp.	1 mL
Granulated sugar — add for dessert crepes only	1 tsp.	5 mL

Beat eggs in large bowl until frothy. Add rest of ingredients. Beat smooth. Cover and store in refrigerator overnight or at least a few hours. Add milk before cooking if too thick. Pour 2 tbsp. (30 mL) in greased hot crepe pan. Tip pan to swirl batter all over pan bottom. Remove when underside is lightly browned. Stack with wax paper in between each crêpe. Secure in plastic bag to store. Use as needed. Makes 24 crêpes.

FRENCH TOAST

Have your eggs and toast all in one.

Eggs	3	3
Granulated sugar	1 tsp.	5 mL
Salt	½ tsp.	2 mL
Milk	¾ cup	175 mL
Stale bread slices	8-10	8-10
Icing sugar for sprinkling		

In mixing bowl put eggs, sugar, salt and milk. Mix together thoroughly.

Dip bread slices in batter. Fry on lightly greased medium hot pan. Brown both sides.

Serve sprinkled with icing sugar if you want to make it extra special. Pass the butter and maple syrup.

Just the right accompaniment to serve with fish.

White corn meal (or yellow)	1½ cups	375 mL
All purpose flour	½ cup	125 mL
Baking powder	3 tsp.	15 mL
Salt	¾ tsp	5 mL
Granulated sugar	1 tsp.	5 mL
Finely grated onion	3 tbsp.	50 mL
Egg	1	1
Milk	¾ cup	175 mL

Fat for deep frying

Measure corn meal, flour, baking powder, salt, sugar and onions into bowl. Stir well to mix evenly.

In another bowl beat egg until frothy. Stir in milk. Pour into dry ingredients. Stir to blend well. Allow to stand until mixture firms up a bit. Drop by small spoonfuls into hot fat or oil 375°F (190°C) until browned. Drain on paper towels. Serve hot. Makes 2 dozen hush puppies.

WAFFLES

A breakfast or brunch treat. Topped with fruit and ice cream makes a welcome dessert.

All purpose flour	1½ cups	375 mL
Granulated sugar	2 tbsp.	30 mL
Baking powder	1 tbsp.	15 mL
Salt	½ tsp.	2 mL
Eggs, beaten	2	2
Milk	1½ cups	375 mL
Melted butter or margarine	¼ cup	50 mL

Put flour, sugar, baking powder and salt into mixing bowl. Stir very well. Make a well in center.

Beat eggs well until frothy in separate bowl. Stir in milk and butter. Pour into well. Beat only until smooth. Fill hot waffle iron according to its instructions. Bake until it stops steaming.

Serve immediately with butter and syrup. Serves 3-4.

Pictured on page 125.

FRITTER BATTER

With a deep fryer you can easily make all kinds of delicious fritters. Sprinkle with sugar for an extra touch.

All purpose flour	1⅓ cups	325 mL
Granulated sugar	2 tbsp.	30 mL
Baking powder	2 tsp.	10 mL
Salt	¼ tsp.	2 mL
Egg	1	1
Milk	¾ cup	175 mL

In mixing bowl put flour, sugar, baking powder and salt.

Beat egg in small bowl until frothy. Add egg and milk to flour mixture. Mix together. Here is where you may have to adjust things. Batter should be thick enough to coat the piece of fruit. If too thin, it runs off. Add more flour to thicken or more milk to thin. When using small pieces like raspberries or drained fruit cocktail, batter has to be thin enough to fold in fruit yet thick enough to hold together. Drop into hot fat 375°F (190°C). Brown each side. Drain on paper towels.

APPLE FRITTERS: Peel and core apples. Cut in rings ½ inch (1 cm) thick or in wedges. Dust with flour. Dip in batter. Cook in 375°F (190°C) fat until browned on both sides. Drain on paper towels.

BANANA FRITTERS: Peel and cut bananas in chunks. Dip in batter. Cook in 375°F (190°C) fat until browned.

CORN FRITTERS: Omit sugar in fritter batter. Stir in 1½ cups (375 mL) cooked kernel corn. Proceed as above.

TOMATO FRITTERS: Omit sugar in fritter batter. Slice very firm tomatoes, green or barely ripe, about ½ inch (1 cm) thick. Dip in batter and proceed as above.

VEGETABLE FRITTERS: Half cook parsnips, carrots and cauliflower chunks. Cool. Dip in batter and proceed as above.

Pictured on page 71.

WELSH CAKES

If you've never tried these, you will wonder why you haven't. Can be served with cheese, jam or butter or rolled in sugar when hot.

All purpose flour	2 cups	500 mL
Granulated sugar	½ cup	125 mL
Baking powder	2 tsp.	10 mL
Salt	½ tsp.	2 mL
Nutmeg	¼ tsp.	1 mL
Cinnamon	¼ tsp.	1 mL
Butter or margarine	½ cup	125 mL
Currants	½ cup	125 mL
Mixed peel	¼ cup	50 mL
Egg	1	1
Milk	⅓ cup	75 mL

Using large bowl, put flour, sugar, baking powder, salt, nutmeg and cinnamon. Cut in butter until crumbly. Stir in currants and peel.

Beat egg with fork. Add egg and milk. Stir into dough as for pie crust. Roll ¼ inch (⅔ cm) thick on floured surface. Cut into 3 inch (7cm) rounds. Fry in frying pan over medium heat browning both sides. To test pan for heat, drops of water should sizzle but not bounce around on pan. Makes 2 dozen or more if smaller rounds are cut.

Pictured on page 71.

FOOLPROOF DOUGHNUTS

You can double or triple this in no time. Tastes like the real thing.

Refrigerated biscuits	1 can of 10
Lard or oil for deep frying, 4-6 inches (15 cm) deep	

Pierce a hole through the center of each biscuit. Shape into flat doughnut. Fry in deep fryer at 375°F (190°C). Brown both sides. Drain on paper towels. Dip in granulated sugar or leave plain. Yield: 10.

CHOCOLATE DOUGHNUTS

Just as easy as plain ones to make. Superb doughnuts.

Cooking oil	3 tbsp.	50 mL
Granulated sugar	1 cup	250 mL
Eggs	2	2
Milk	1 cup	250 mL
Vanilla	1 tsp.	5 mL
All purpose flour	3¾ cups	925 mL
Baking powder	4 tsp.	20 mL
Salt	½ tsp.	3 mL
Cocoa	⅓ cup	75 mL

Lard or oil for deep frying.

Put oil, sugar, eggs, milk and vanilla in mixing bowl. Mix together well.

Add flour, baking powder, salt and cocoa. Stir to blend. Heat lard to 375°F (190°C).

On floured surface roll dough ¼ inch (⅝ cm) thick. Cut with doughnut cutter. Drop carefully into hot fat a few at a time so as not to crowd. When light brown turn to cook other side. Cook center "holes" too. Drain standing on edge, on paper towels on tray. Glaze for special effect. Makes 2 dozen.

GLAZE: Mix enough milk with 1 cup (250 mL) icing sugar and ¼ cup (50 mL) cocoa to make a fairly thick runny icing. Dip top side of doughnuts. Dry on tray.

Pictured on page 71.

Watch everyone gather around for the big fry.

Melted butter or margarine	3 tbsp.	50 mL
Granulated sugar	1 cup	250 mL
Eggs	2	2
Milk	1 cup	250 mL
Vanilla	1 tsp.	5 mL
All purpose flour	4 cups	1 L
Baking powder	4 tsp.	20 mL
Salt	½ tsp.	2 mL
Cinnamon	½ tsp.	2 mL
Nutmeg	½ tsp.	2 mL

Lard or oil for deep frying, 4-6 inches (10-15 cm) deep.

In mixing bowl combine melted butter, sugar, eggs, milk and vanilla. Mix together.

Measure in flour, baking powder, salt, cinnamon and nutmeg. Stir well. Heat lard to 375°F (190°C).

Roll out dough ¼ inch thick on floured surface. Cut out with doughnut cutter. Drop into hot fat a few at a time so as not to crowd. Turn when light brown to cook other side. Fry "holes" too. Remove to tray standing on edge on paper towels to cool. If you like your doughnuts sugared, put them with ¼ cup (50 mL) granulated sugar in paper bag and shake. For cinnamon flavor, add ¼ tsp. (3 mL) cinnamon to sugar in bag. Makes 3 dozen.

Note: If you long for the taste of doughnuts yet you can't eat fried foods, bake some in 350°F (180°C) oven for 20-30 minutes.

Pictured on page 71.

ORANGE DOUGHNUTS: Add 2 tbsp. (30 mL) finely grated orange rind to batter.

GLAZE: Mix enough orange juice with 1 cup (250 mL) icing sugar to make thin icing. Dip top side of doughnuts into icing. Dry on tray.

BROWN SUGAR GLAZE

Brown sugar	5 tbsp.	75 mL
Butter or margarine	2 tbsp.	30 mL
Cream or milk	2 tbsp.	30 mL
Crushed nuts	1-2 tbsp.	15-30 mL

Combine sugar, butter and cream in small saucepan. Bring to boil and simmer for 3 minutes. Spoon over hot loaf. Sprinkle with nuts. Especially good spread over Poppy Seed Loaf and Date Loaf.

BUTTER NUT SPREAD

Butter or margarine	½ cup	125 mL
Grated orange peel	1 tbsp.	15 mL
Hazelnuts, finely chopped	½ cup	125 mL

Beat butter until fluffy. Mix in orange peel and nuts. Try it with several loaves.

CINNAMON BUTTER

Softened butter or margarine	½ cup	125 mL
Packed brown sugar	¾ cup	175 mL
Milk	2 tbsp.	30 mL
Cinnamon	1½ tsp.	7 mL

Beat until blended and fluffy. Good with hot breads and muffins.

FRUITED CHEESE

Mash small package cream cheese with any fruit such as peaches, raspberries, pineapple or strawberries.

CLEAR GLAZE

Corn syrup	½ cup	125 mL
Water	¼ cup	50 mL

Bring syrup and water to boil in saucepan. Spoon over loaf. It dries clear and shiny. Dresses up any loaf.

CREAM CHEESE SPREAD

Cream cheese (small pkg.)	½ cup	125 mL
Butter or margarine	2 tbsp.	30 mL
Vanilla	¾ tsp.	5 mL
Icing sugar	¾ cup	175 mL
Finely chopped pecans	¼ cup	50 mL

Beat together well the cheese, butter, vanilla and icing sugar. Stir in nuts.

CREAMED LEMON CHEESE

Cream cheese, small pkg.	1	1
Lemon juice	1 tbsp.	15 mL
Grated lemon rind	1 tsp.	5 mL

Beat all together well. Use as a spread.

LEMON GLAZE

Lemon juice	3 tbsp.	50 mL
Granulated sugar	¼ cup	50 mL

Bring to boil. Stir to dissolve. Spoon over loaf or muffins. Good over zucchini loaf.

ORANGE CREAM SPREAD

Cream cheese	½ cup	125 mL
Frozen concentrated orange juice	3 tbsp.	50 mL
Granulated sugar	1 tbsp.	15 mL

Mix until smooth. Use to spread on date, pumpkin, raisin, apple, ginger, orange and peanut butter loaves.

ORANGE GLAZE

Orange juice of orange	1	1
Granulated sugar	¼ cup	50 mL

Heat and stir in small saucepan to dissolve sugar. Spoon over loaves or muffins.

PROCESSED CHEESE SPREAD

Use directly from bottle to spread on slices from loaves such as Date Loaf, Raisin, Apple and any you feel like trying.

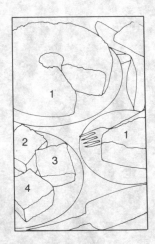

1. Cranberry Coffee Cake page 147
2. Choco Coffee Cake page 149
3. Apple Coffee Cake page 146
4. Streusel Coffee Cake page 150

PUMPKIN GLAZE

Icing sugar	½ cup	125 mL
Cinnamon	⅛ tsp.	½ mL
Nutmeg	⅛ tsp.	½ mL
Cream or milk	1-2 tbsp.	15-30 mL

Beat all together. Spread over loaf. Just made for pumpkin loaves.

STRAWBERRY CREAM

| Cream cheese | ½ cup | 125 mL |
| Strawberry jam | ¼-½ cup | 50-125 mL |

Beat together well. Use as a spread.

STRAWBERRY BUTTER

Butter or margarine	½ cup	125 mL
Strawberry jam	½ cup	125 mL
Fresh strawberries, mashed	½ cup	125 mL

Beat butter until soft and fluffy. Add jam and beat well. Mix in mashed strawberries. Serve with plain muffins. Try with several other muffins, biscuits and loaves. Extra delicious.

VANILLA GLAZE

Icing sugar	1 cup	250 mL
Water	3-4 tsp.	15-20 mL
Vanilla	½ tsp.	2 mL
Grated nuts	½ cup	125 mL

Beat together well. Spread over loaf of your choice.

APPLE COFFEE CAKE

What an aroma with which to greet your coffee company!

All purpose flour	1⅓ cups	325 mL
Granulated sugar	¾ cup	175 mL
Baking powder	3 tsp.	15 mL
Salt	¼ tsp.	2 mL
Butter or margarine	¼ cup	50 mL
Egg, beaten	1	1
Milk	¾ cup	175 mL
Vanilla	1 tsp.	5 mL
Cooking apples, peeled and sliced	2	2

TOPPING

| Packed brown sugar | ⅓ cup | 75 mL |
| Cinnamon | ½ tsp. | 3 mL |

Put flour, sugar, baking powder and salt in large bowl. Cut or rub in butter until crumbly. Make a well in the center.

In another bowl beat egg until frothy. Mix in milk and vanilla. Pour into well. Stir just enough to moisten. Pour into greased 8 × 8 inch (20 × 20 cm) cake pan. Push apples well into batter close together.

TOPPING

Mix brown sugar and cinnamon together and sprinkle over top. Bake in 350°F (180°C) oven for 50-60 minutes until it begins to shrink from edge of pan. Serves 9.

Pictured on page 143.

Whether you try cranberries, raspberries or blueberries you will have a very colorful treat.

All purpose flour	2 cups	500 mL
Granulated sugar	½ cup	125 mL
Baking powder	3 tsp.	15 mL
Salt	½ tsp.	2 mL
Eggs	2	2
Cooking oil	¼ cup	50 mL
Milk	¾ cup	175 mL
Cranberries, fresh or frozen	1 cup	250 mL
TOPPING:		
All purpose flour	⅓ cup	75 mL
Packed brown sugar	⅓ cup	75 mL
Butter or margarine	¼ cup	50 mL
Cinnamon	1 tsp.	5 mL

Mix flour, sugar, baking powder and salt together in mixing bowl.

In another bowl beat eggs until frothy. Mix in oil and milk. Pour into dry ingredients. Mix together. Fold in cranberries. Scrape into greased 9 inch (23 cm) tube pan.

TOPPING: Mix flour, brown sugar, butter and cinnamon together. Sprinkle over top of batter. Bake in 350°F (180°C) oven for 50-60 minutes or until it begins to shrink away from sides of pan. Cool about 30 minutes before removing from pan. Turn right side up.

BLUEBERRY COFFEE CAKE: Omit cranberries. Add 1 cup (250 mL) blueberries, fresh or frozen.

RASPBERRY COFFEE CAKE: Omit cranberries. Add 1 cup (250 mL) raspberries.

Pictured on page 143.

SOUR CREAM COFFEE CAKE

A favorite cinnamony coffee cake.

Butter or margarine, softened	½ cup	125 mL
Granulated sugar	1 cup	250 mL
Eggs	2	2
Baking soda	1 tsp.	5 mL
Sour cream	1 cup	250 mL
All purpose flour	1½ cups	375 mL
Baking powder	1½ tsp.	7 mL
Salt	¼ tsp.	1 mL
Packed brown sugar	½ cup	125 mL
Cinnamon	1 tsp.	5 mL
Finely chopped nuts	½ cup	125 mL

Cream butter, sugar and 1 egg together well in mixing bowl. Beat in second egg. Add soda and sour cream. Mix.

Mix flour, baking powder and salt together. Add to batter. Stir to mix. Put one half batter in greased 9 × 9 inch (22 × 22 cm) pan.

Mix brown sugar, cinnamon and nuts together. Sprinkle one half over batter. Spoon second half of batter here and there over top. Sprinkle second half of cinnamon mixture over all. Bake in 350°F (180°C) oven for 45 minutes or until an inserted toothpick comes out clean. Serve warm.

And where else do old Volkswagens go but to the old Volk's home?

No cinnamon in this. Delicious chocolate chips instead.

Butter or margarine	½ cup	125 mL
Granulated sugar	1 cup	250 mL
Eggs	2	2
Vanilla	1 tsp.	5 mL
All purpose flour	2 cups	500 mL
Baking powder	1 tsp.	5 mL
Baking soda	1 tsp.	5 mL
Sour Cream	1 cup	250 mL
Semi-sweet chocolate chips	½ cup	125 mL

TOPPING

Packed brown sugar	½ cup	125 mL
All purpose flour	½ cup	125 mL
Cocoa	2 tsp.	10 mL
Butter or margarine	¼ cup	50 mL
Semi-sweet chocolate chips	½ cup	125 mL
Finely chopped nuts	½ cup	125 mL

In mixing bowl cream butter, sugar and 1 egg together well. Beat in second egg and vanilla. Add flour, baking powder, soda and sour cream. Beat to mix. Stir in chips. Turn into greased 9 × 13 inch pan (22 × 33 cm). Smooth top.

TOPPING: Mix brown sugar, flour, cocoa and butter together until crumbly. Stir in chips and nuts. Sprinkle over top of batter. Bake in 350°F (180°C) oven for 45 minutes until an inserted toothpick comes out clean.

Pictured on page 143.

Most kids who put a tooth under their pillow find a dime in the morning. Johnny found a dollar. It pays to have buck teeth.

STREUSEL COFFEE CAKE

A good reliable stand-by. Easy to make for company "on the way".

Butter or margarine, softened	⅓ cup	75 mL
Granulated sugar	½ cup	125 mL
Egg	1	1
All purpose flour	1½ cups	350 mL
Baking powder	2 tsp.	10 mL
Salt	½ tsp.	2 mL
Milk	¾ cup	175 mL

TOPPING

Brown sugar, packed	½ cup	125 mL
All purpose flour	2 tbsp.	30 mL
Cinnamon	1 tsp.	5 mL
Butter or margarine, melted	3 tbsp.	50 mL

Cream butter, sugar and egg together well in mixing bowl.

Stir flour, baking powder and salt together.

Measure out milk. Add alternately with flour mixture. Scrape into greased 9 × 9 inch (22 × 22 cm) pan. Smooth top.

TOPPING: Mix brown sugar, flour, cinnamon and melted butter together. Using fingers for easy distribution, sprinkle over batter. Bake in 375°F (190°C) oven for about 35 minutes until an inserted toothpick comes out clean. Serve warm.

Pictured on page 143.

ORANGE STREUSEL COFFEE CAKE: Omit cinnamon in topping and add 1 tbsp. (15 mL) grated orange rind.

FRUITED COFFEE CAKE: Add ¼ cup (50 mL) each of glazed mixed fruit, currants and raisins. For Topping use only the brown sugar and cinnamon.

METRIC CONVERSION

Throughout this book measurements are given in conventional and metric measure. To compensate for differences between the two measurements due to rounding, a full metric measure is not always used.

The cup used is the standard 8 fluid ounce.

Temperature is given in degrees Fahrenheit and Celsius.

Baking pan measurements are in inches and centimetres, as well as quarts and litres. An exact conversion is given below as well as the working equivalent.

Spoons	Exact Conversion	Standard Metric Measure
¼ teaspoon	1.2 millilitres	1 millilitre
½ teaspoon	2.4 millilitres	2 millilitres
1 teaspoon	4.7 millilitres	5 millilitres
2 teaspoons	9.4 millilitres	10 millilitres
1 tablespoon	14.2 millilitres	15 millilitres

Cups		
¼ cup (4 T)	56.8 millilitres	50 millilitres
⅓ cup (5⅓ T)	75.6 millilitres	75 millilitres
½ cup (8 T)	113.7 millilitres	125 millilitres
⅔ cup (10⅔ T)	151.2 millilitres	150 millilitres
¾ cup (12 T)	170.5 millilitres	175 millilitres
1 cup (16 T)	227.3 millilitres	250 millilitres
4½ cups	984.8 millilitres	1000 millilitres, 1 litre

Ounces — Weight		
1 oz.	28.3 grams	30 grams
2 oz.	56.7 grams	55 grams
3 oz.	85 grams	85 grams
4 oz.	113.4 grams	125 grams
5 oz.	141.7 grams	140 grams
6 oz.	170.1 grams	170 grams
7 oz.	198.4 grams	200 grams
8 oz.	226.8 grams	250 grams
16 oz.	453.6 grams	500 grams
32 oz.	917.2 grams	1000 grams, 1 kg

Pans, Casseroles

8 × 8 inch, 20 × 20 cm, 2L
9 × 9 inch, 22 × 22 cm, 2.5L
9 × 13 inch, 22 × 33 cm, 4L
10 × 15 inch, 25 × 38 cm, 1.2L
11 × 17 inch, 28 × 43 cm, 1.5L

8 × 2 inch round, 20 × 5 cm, 2L
9 × 2 inch round, 22 × 5 cm, 2.5L
10 × 4½ inch tube, 25 × 11 cm, 5L
8 × 4 × 3 inch loaf, 20 × 10 × 7 cm, 1.5L
9 × 5 × 3 inch loaf, 23 × 12 × 7 cm, 2L

Oven Temperatures

Fahrenheit	Celsius	Fahrenheit	Celsius	Fahrenheit	Celsius
175°	80°	300°	150°	425°	220°
200°	100°	325°	160°	450°	230°
225°	110°	350°	180°	475°	240°
250°	120°	375°	190°	500°	260°
275°	140°	400°	200°		

INDEX

(continued on next page)

(continued on next page)

(continued on next page)

(continued on next page)

COOKBOOKS

COMPANY'S COMING
PUBLISHING LIMITED
BOX 8037, STATION "F"
EDMONTON, ALBERTA,
CANADA T6H 4N9

SAVE $5.00!

Please send the following cookbooks to the address on the reverse side of this coupon.

TITLE (Soft Cover)	QTY.	EACH	TOTAL
150 DELICIOUS SQUARES (Also available in French – see below)		$9.95	
CASSEROLES		$9.95	
MUFFINS & MORE		$9.95	
SALADS		$9.95	
APPETIZERS		$9.95	
DESSERTS		$9.95	
SOUPS & SANDWICHES		$9.95	
HOLIDAY ENTERTAINING		$9.95	
COOKIES		$9.95	
VEGETABLES		$9.95	
MAIN COURSES		$9.95	
PASTA		$9.95	
CAKES		$9.95	
BARBECUES (April, 1991)		$9.95	
TITLE (Hard Cover)			
JEAN PARÉ'S FAVORITES VOLUME ONE – 232 pages		$17.95	
TITLE (Soft Cover) French			
150 DÉLICIEUX CARRÉS		$9.95	
	TOTAL QUANTITY		TOTAL COST OF BOOKS $

Plus $1.00 postage and handling **per book**	$
Less $5.00 for every third book per order	_ $
Plus international shipping expenses (**Add** $4.00 if outside Canada or USA)	$
Plus tax if applicable	$
Total amount enclosed:	$

SPECIAL MAIL OFFER:
Order any 2 cookbooks by mail at regular prices and **save $5.00** on every third cookbook per order.

Prices subject to change after December 31, 1992. *Sorry, no C.O.D.s.*

ORDERS OUTSIDE CANADA:
Amount enclosed must be in US funds.

MAKE CHEQUE OR MONEY ORDER PAYABLE TO;
Company's Coming Publishing Limited Box 8037, Station F Edmonton, Alberta Canada, T6H 4N9

↓ GIFT CARD MESSAGE ↓

COOKBOOKS

A GIFT FOR YOU

COOKBOOKS

A NATIONAL **BEST SELLER**

I would like to order the Company's Coming Cookbooks listed on the reverse side of this coupon.

NAME_____
(PLEASE PRINT

STREET_____

CITY _____

PROVINCE/STATE _____ POSTAL CODE/ZIP _____

GIFT GIVING – WE MAKE IT EASY...
... YOU MAKE IT DELICIOUS!

Let us help you with your gift giving! We will send cookbooks directly to the recipients of your choice if you give us their names and addresses. Be sure to specify the titles of the cookbooks you wish to send to each person.

Enclose a personal note or card for each gift or use our handy gift card below.

Company's Coming Cookbooks are the perfect gift for birthdays, showers, Mother's Day, Father's Day, graduation or any occasion ... collect them all!

Don't forget to take advantage of the **$5.00 saving ... buy any two Company's Coming Cookbooks by mail and save $5.00 on every third copy per order.**

↓ GIFT CARD MESSAGE ↓

COOKBOOKS

COMPANY'S COMING
PUBLISHING LIMITED
BOX 8037, STATION "F"
EDMONTON, ALBERTA,
CANADA T6H 4N9

SAVE $5.00!

Please send the following cookbooks to the address on the reverse side of this coupon.

TITLE (Soft Cover)	QTY.	EACH	TOTAL
150 DELICIOUS SQUARES (Also available in French – see below)		$9.95	
CASSEROLES		$9.95	
MUFFINS & MORE		$9.95	
SALADS		$9.95	
APPETIZERS		$9.95	
DESSERTS		$9.95	
SOUPS & SANDWICHES		$9.95	
HOLIDAY ENTERTAINING		$9.95	
COOKIES		$9.95	
VEGETABLES		$9.95	
MAIN COURSES		$9.95	
PASTA		$9.95	
CAKES		$9.95	
BARBECUES (April, 1991)		$9.95	
TITLE (Hard Cover)			
JEAN PARÉ'S FAVORITES VOLUME ONE – 232 pages		$17.95	
TITLE (Soft Cover) French			
150 DÉLICIEUX CARRÉS		$9.95	
	TOTAL QUANTITY		TOTAL COST OF BOOKS $

Plus $1.00 postage and handling **per book**	$
Less $5.00 for every third book per order	– $
Plus international shipping expenses (**Add $4.00** if outside Canada or USA)	$
Plus tax if applicable	$
Total amount enclosed:	$

**SPECIAL
MAIL OFFER:**
Order any 2 cook-
books by mail at
regular prices and
save $5.00 on
every third cook-
book per order.

Prices subject to
change after
December 31, 1992.
Sorry, no C.O.D.s.

**ORDERS
OUTSIDE CANADA:**
Amount enclosed
must be in
US funds.

**MAKE CHEQUE
OR MONEY
ORDER PAYABLE
TO:**
Company's Coming
Publishing Limited
Box 8037, Station F
Edmonton, Alberta
Canada, T6H 4N9

↓ **GIFT CARD MESSAGE** ↓

COOKBOOKS

A GIFT FOR YOU

COOKBOOKS

I would like to order the Company's Coming Cookbooks listed on the reverse side of this coupon.

NAME_____
(PLEASE PRINT)

STREET_____

CITY _____

PROVINCE/STATE _____ POSTAL CODE/ZIP _____

GIFT GIVING – WE MAKE IT EASY...
... YOU MAKE IT DELICIOUS!

Let us help you with your gift giving! We will send cookbooks directly to the recipients of your choice if you give us their names and addresses. Be sure to specify the titles of the cookbooks you wish to send to each person.

Enclose a personal note or card for each gift or use our handy gift card below.

Company's Coming Cookbooks are the perfect gift for birthdays, showers, Mother's Day, Father's Day, graduation or any occasion ... collect them all!

Don't forget to take advantage of the **$5.00 saving ... buy any two Company's Coming Cookbooks by mail and save $5.00 on every third copy per order.**

↓ GIFT CARD MESSAGE ↓